Praying *in* Pregnancy

Cradling Your Baby
in God's Promises

MARIE LYNCH

Title: Praying in Pregnancy / Marie Lynch
Copyright 2025 by Marie Lynch.
Published by 68:11 Press.

For permission requests or information about special discounts for bulk purchases, contact 68:11 Press at perfectlyknit@gmail.com.

Unless otherwise noted, all Scripture quotations are from The Holy Bible, English Standard Version ® (ESV ®), copyright © 2001 by Crossway, a publishing ministry of Good News Publishers. Used by permission. All rights reserved.

Scripture quotations marked (AMP) are taken from *The Amplified ® Bible*, Copyright © 1954, 1958, 1962, 1964, 1965, 1987, by the Lockman Foundation. Used by permission. (www.Lockman.org.) All rights reserved.

Scripture quotations marked (NIV) are taken from the Holy Bible, New International Version®, NIV®. Copyright © 1973, 1978, 1984, 2011 by Biblica, Inc.™ Used by permission of Zondervan. All rights reserved worldwide. www.zondervan.com. The "NIV" and "New International Version" are trademarks registered in the United States Patent and Trademark Office by Biblica, Inc.™

Book design (cover and interior) by Inksnatcher.com, with cover concept by the author.

Subjects: | BISAC: RELIGION/Prayer. RELIGION/Christian Living / Family. FAMILY & RELATIONSHIPS / Parenting / Pregnancy & Childbirth.

Description: First edition. | 68:11 Press, 2025. | Summary: "*Praying in Pregnancy* is a heartfelt prayer devotional that guides expectant moms in bonding with their baby, growing in faith, and finding peace through daily prayers and reflections." —Provided by 68:11 Press.

Identifiers: ISBN 979-8-9918049-4-3 (softcover B&W interior) | 979-8-9918049-0-5 (softcover) | 979-8-9918049-1-2 (hardcover) | 979-8-9918049-2-9 (e-book)

Printed in the United States of America.

To Brad, who gave me four precious reasons to write this book.

contents

First Trimester

Second Trimester

Third Trimester

weeks one and two

Pregnancy is counted from the first day of the last menstrual period, so during these first two weeks of your nine months of pregnancy, God is already at work preparing your body to be your baby's first temporary home. A follicle-stimulating hormone (FSH) is helping your ovarian follicles develop, and one of these follicles will eventually prepare to release an egg that God has been maturing. After your period ends, the lining of your uterus will regenerate and thicken again in preparation for a potential pregnancy. Your estrogen levels will start to rise gradually, which also helps with conception. All of these inner workings of your body are unseen and unfelt. God alone sees these processes, designing them well before you (or a doctor) can detect a pregnancy. He is *amazing* in His creative love!

WEEK

three

day 15   knit

Congratulations! You are officially pregnant. Today, your egg was host to a sperm, creating life. Amazingly, DNA came together and has become the blueprint of another human life. Only God could orchestrate such a beautiful miracle. In the same way, your child will be embedded with the DNA of their heavenly Father, carrying and bearing His image on the earth.

Praise God, who is right now fashioning and forming your little one into His image (Genesis 1:27).

Thank the Father for forming your baby's mind, body, and spirit perfectly (Psalm 139:13-15; Isaiah 51:16).

Meditate on the Lord's awesome love for your child (Psalm 139:18; Isaiah 49:1, 16).

Momma,

You will have fresh revelation of the Father's love with each day of prayer and meditation in this book. You will see the incredible detail and nurturing He has not just for your little one but also for you. Let His fiery love set you ablaze with passion for Him and burn up all unbelief. You are so carefully knit together, beloved.

day 16 called

Amazingly, the gender of your baby has already been determined. Sperm are fascinating creations carrying X (girl) or Y (boy) chromosomes. The Father's grand design of humanity was to create male and female for His glory and purposes. Each gender has unique traits that distinguish one from the other.

Pray that your child walks as a beloved son or daughter of God who is secure in their identity.

Meditate on Isaiah 43:1-7, noting all the ways God is so personally and intimately acquainted with your child.

This is what the LORD says—he who created you, Jacob, he who formed you, Israel: "... I have summoned you by name; you are mine. When you pass through the waters, I will be with you; and when you pass through the rivers, they will not sweep over you. When you walk through the fire, you will not be burned; the flames will not set you ablaze. For I am the LORD your God, the Holy One of Israel, your Savior; ... you are precious and honored in my sight, ... Do not be afraid, for I am with you; ... Bring my sons from afar and my daughters from the ends of the earth—everyone who is called by my name, whom I created for my glory, whom I formed and made."

Beloved,

You were handpicked, hand designed, and perfectly chosen to carry this child. No one will be a better momma to your baby than you. Trust God's will, including His perfect timing, as you walk through this pregnancy. He longs for you to experience His goodness. See how He parents you—full of tender mercy and compassion.

day 17   kingdom carrier

Today, your egg will divide into more cells, and these will settle at the top of your uterus. Your baby's life will continue to increase and develop until the day of their birth. This increase is also symbolic of the life of your child advancing the kingdom of God. One life can have an eternal influence in spreading the gospel across the earth.

Pray your child will be a kingdom carrier.

Ask God to fill your child with bold love, always ready to give a reason for the hope they have (1 Peter 3:15).

Pray that your son or daughter will not be ashamed of the gospel, because they will know it is the power of God that brings salvation to everyone who believes (Romans 1:16).

Ask the Father to use your child to turn the world upside down for the kingdom of God (Acts 17:6).

Momma,

How incredible and humbling that God chose you to be the carrier of His heart, the spirit of His very Son. You are representing Him on the earth by showing people what He is like. You walk as He did: filled with His love, empowered by His Spirit, and abiding with the Father (1 John 2:6). The world needs to see Him in you, Momma.

# day 18 secret place

Today, your baby is only known by the Father. A pregnancy test cannot detect your pregnancy for a few weeks, so you are likely reading these early pages to catch up, now that you know you are with child. What a beautiful thought to know your baby was in the secret place, only known by their creator.

Begin to pray that your child will live from a place of deep intimacy with God.

Bless your child, who will dwell in the shelter of the Most High and will abide in the shadow of the Almighty (Psalm 91:1).

Pray that your child will experience power in the secret place (Matthew 6:6) as they abide in the true Vine (John 15).

Ask the Father to give your son or daughter a heart that always declares "I will say to the LORD, 'My refuge and my fortress, my God, in whom I trust'" (Psalm 91:2).

Momma,

Become a lover of God's presence. He will change you just by your soaking in His stillness. The power of His presence leaves you wholly changed, healed, set free, and strengthened. Oftentimes, you do not have to say a word! His glory manifests as you seek Him.

day 19 transition

Today, the ball of cells called the blastula is continuing to multiply and is ready to settle at home for the next nine months in your uterine wall. Similarly, your baby will soon settle in your physical home. Becoming a parent is one of the most exciting transitions in life. Parenthood is a gift from the best parent—God Himself. Praise the Father for His grace as He teaches you how to love like Him.

Rejoice in God for the way He is making you grow in this season. "But now, O LORD, you are our Father; we are the clay, and you are our potter; we are all the work of Your hand" (Isaiah 64:8).

Pray God will give you His very heart and compassion as you become a mother. Just as fathers have compassion on their children, so the Lord has compassion on those who fear Him (Psalm 103:3).

Confess your need for the Spirit's wisdom and thank Him that He loves to give you more of Himself (Luke 11:13).

Beloved, you were created in God's own image. He designed His creation to "be fruitful and multiply and fill the earth" (Genesis 1:28) because He wants to multiply His image on the earth. Imagine the whole world full of people who are like God! He says to your heart today, "Do not fear parenthood." He will give you His Spirit, empowering you with love in every mistake and victory.

day 20 overcomer

Hormones are being released in your body that will sustain your pregnancy. In the same way God supplies these natural pregnancy supporters, He gives you His Holy Spirit to maintain victory in an overcoming life. As you learn more and more about pregnant life, so, too, will you learn about God's goodness in this season.

Give thanks to the Father, who gives you the victory through Jesus Christ (1 Corinthians 15:57).

Beloved, you are an overcomer through faith (1 John 5:4).

As you parent your little one, you will be more than a conqueror through Jesus, who loves you (Romans 8:37). Thank Him for the victory He has already given you.

You have nothing to fear because the One who is in you is greater than the one who is in the world (the devil) (1 John 4:4).

He finishes every good work He has planned for both you and your child (Philippians 1:6).

Momma,

How can you ever lose? You have all of God living inside you. He gives you everything you need: wisdom, strength, and power to love Him above all things, including your child. As you love Him, He will supply you with an overflow of love for others. Confess any unbelief or fear you may have today. Draw from His endless well of love. Soak in His empowering presence because it can never be exhausted.

day 27   hidden

Your blastula, or baby cell ball, is getting fixed into a place where the blood flow increases, making way for the placenta. You may be unaware of your pregnancy at this early stage. The Father is a wonderful secret keeper, but He longs to tell you secrets from His heart (Matthew 13:11). As your little one grows, ask Him to reveal the mysteries of the kingdom to you.

Praise God, who promises to bring hidden things to manifestation and concealed things to light (Luke 8:17).

Your baby's total being—body, soul, and spirit—is being knitted together in secret right now (Psalm 139:14). Thank Him today for being such a beautiful designer of life.

As you call on God, He promises to answer you and tell you great and hidden things you haven't known (Jeremiah 33:3).

Momma,

Jesus said it has been given to you to know the secrets of His kingdom. Ask Him what He specifically wants to reveal to your heart today. Write down what He says. Practice the stillness of being in His presence as He speaks.

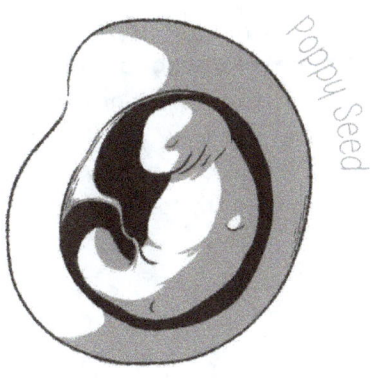

Poppy Seed

WEEK

four

day 22   faith

Although you're pregnant, you cannot see or feel any immediate change yet. What a beautiful illustration of faith. God defines faith as "the conviction of things not seen"(Hebrews 11:1). Over the next nine months, you may not feel many changes happening within your womb, but you can trust God, who sees all. He is El Roi, "the God who sees." Ask Him to grant you pure faith to trust Him through this season.

Meditate and pray through Galatians 2:20: "I have been crucified with Christ. It is no longer I who live, but Christ who lives in me. And the life I now live in the flesh I live by faith in the Son of God, who loved me and gave himself for me."

The way, the truth, and the life resides in your spirit. He wants you to believe Him, even when you cannot see or understand in the natural what is happening. Begin to look with your "faith eyes" and not with your natural sight. You literally walk by faith, not by sight (2 Corinthians 5:7). Hold fast to His promises and His unchanging Word, and do not waver in unbelief (Philippians 2:6).

Momma,

Practice a simple, childlike trust in His goodness toward you. Receive His promise to prosper you and not harm you, to fulfill His plans, and to give you a hope and a future (Jeremiah 29:11). Take His Word and enjoy the freedom He is offering (Galatians 5:1). What do you need, child? He is able.

day 23   precious

God is the creator of life. Whether this is your first pregnancy or tenth, and no matter your station in life—married or not—this baby is wanted. Not only is God the creator of life, but He also loves to give life. The enemy comes to "steal and kill and destroy" (John 10:10), but Jesus comes to give superabundant life to you. You, as well as this child, are so desired by the One who made you.

God says, "How precious to me are your thoughts, O God! How vast is the sum of them!" (Psalm 139:16-17).

He is intimately acquainted with you, even knowing the number of hairs on your head (Matthew 10:30-31). Praise Him because He knows the depths of your heart better than you.

He chose you, beloved. He said of you that you are His, He gave Jesus in exchange for your life (Isaiah 43:4).

Momma,

Respond to God's deep desire of you with, "Lord, I'm yours wholly and completely. I don't withhold any part of my life from you. Come and make yourself at home more and more in the rooms of my heart. Not one door is closed. I trust you with the interior design of each space."

day 24   supply

The womb, where your little one is developing, contains an amniotic sac, also called the membrane. Amniotic fluid keeps the temperature stable and will be a shield of protection should you suffer a fall or a blow to your belly. God is making provisions constantly on your behalf. He has already made a way for protecting this child, and He calls Himself Jehovah Jireh, "the LORD who provides." Rejoice in His perfect provision.

Praise God, who "is able to make all grace abound to you, so that having all sufficiency in all things at all times, you may abound in every good work" (2 Corinthians 9:8).

Declare that His divine power has given you everything you need for a godly life. It's His promise to you in Christ (2 Peter 1:3).

Momma,

What does your heart need most today? Do you need to be soothed, reassured, or simply held? He already knows, beloved. Look up, literally. Go look at the sky and linger in the looking. Gaze at its vastness. Look at the sun or stars and know that the God who made them can hold your heart too.

Journal your thoughts about this today.

day 25   humble

Your little one has crossed over, developing from blastula (cell ball) to embryo. He or she is so tiny, only about the size of a pin dot—one-fifth of a millimeter. Take a pen and put a dot on the page. Your baby is smaller than this. Even though your baby cannot be easily seen, this is God's perfect design of His perfect creation. From tiny seeds come gigantic trees, and so it is with your baby. The seed you carry will advance the unending, vast, limitless kingdom of God on earth.

Meditate on how the Lord purposely uses weak or humble things, like children, to shame the wise of the world (1 Corinthians 1:27). Praise Him for His strength that is displayed and being made perfect in you.

Praise God for the way He uses the natural, the realm you can see, to mirror the supernatural, or unseen, spirit realm. He alone is growing your baby physically, and He alone will be the One who will water the spiritual seed within them. His Spirit is carefully watching over His Word to perform it.

Momma,

Can you sit and fathom the sweet, little life growing inside you right now? They are a perfect illustration of the Christ-life within. As your baby grows because you nourish them, so, too, your inner self-will be strengthened as you feed on the Word through His Spirit. You will feel your spirit rise as you wait and trust His promises. Sometimes this is practiced hour by hour by just abiding in Him. Thank Him today for His humility in coming close to your heart.

day 26   time

Your baby will be born approximately 250 days from today. You are almost six thousand hours away from holding your newborn. What wells up in your heart as you realize this? What you can trust is this: The Lord's timing is perfect. He is the creator of time and holds the heavenly agenda for every appointed event in your life and the life of your child.

This pregnancy is for a season, and when the days seem long, wait on the Lord. Pray for patience, the fruit of His Spirit, and He will make your spirit strong (Psalm 27:14).

Ask the Father for complete trust in Him and His timing, not leaning on your own understanding (Proverbs 3:5).

Thank Him for making all things beautiful in His time (Ecclesiastes 3:11).

Momma,

You, like your baby, are being formed and fashioned into the image of Jesus. You will see as He sees, including the way He perceives time. He is not bound by time, and you shouldn't be either. If you've been ruled by time or are anxious concerning His timing, confess your heart to Him. Thank the Holy Spirit for opening the eyes of your heart to see He is perfect in all His ways. Let His timing astound you and you will see, sooner or later (sometimes much later), that He alone knows when and how to answer the cry of your heart.

day 27   awesome

Your pregnancy still cannot be registered through an over-the-counter test, but your baby can be spotted by an ultrasound, a more specialized method of spying into the womb. Isn't it amazing to think of God's all-knowing power? He is completely aware of all things, even when we are not. The omnipotence and greatness of God cannot be compared to anyone or anything.

He is the God who sees. Praise the Lord, who said, "With man it is impossible, but not with God. For all things are possible with God" (Mark 10:27). Insert your "impossibility" here _____, and repent of your unbelief. He longs to give you not just faith of your own, but that of His divine nature, the very faith of Jesus.

Rejoice in His greatness. He is not only on your side, but He is also inside. Declare, "Yours, O LORD, is the greatness and the power and the glory and the victory and the majesty, for all that is in the heavens and in the earth is yours. Yours is the kingdom, O LORD, and you are exalted as head above all" (1 Chronicles 29:11).

Momma,

Spill your heart before Him. Maybe His greatness came close today in a small, tangible way. Jot down your very own love song or praise to Him in your journal.

day 28   gift

You may be experiencing signs of pregnancy, like a missed period. You might have known from conception, or you may be wondering if your period is just late. Think of God's smile when He reveals to you this precious little one He has prepared just for you. He is the giver of all good gifts (James 1:17). Just like He gives you gifts in the natural, He desires to give you spiritual gifts as well. What gifts has He blessed you with?

Ask God to give you "spirit eyes" to see His goodness in all things, especially in the challenging circumstances of your life. He promises all things work together for good as you love Him and walk in your calling (Romans 8:28).

Pray this scripture over your child, blessing them in the Lord: Sweet child, may "The LORD bless you and keep you; the LORD make his face to shine upon you and be gracious to you; the LORD lift up his countenance upon you and give you peace" (Numbers 6:24-26). Amen.

Momma,

Live from expectation always of God's love and goodness toward you. He delights in your expectation, your hope, and your anticipation of what He will be for you in each season. Dream and think big. He has more for you than you can imagine in Christ (Ephesians 3:20).

Apple Seed

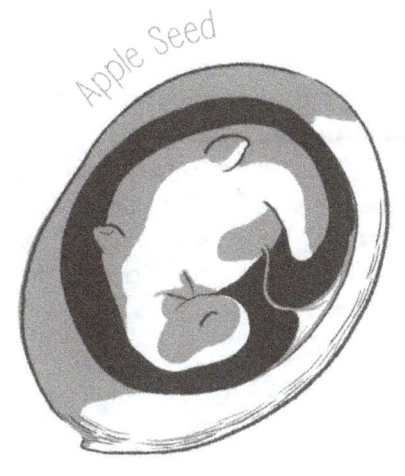

WEEK

five

day 29 — designed

Baby embryos multiply cells specific to the major functions of their little bodies. Some of the functions include the skeletal system, the nervous system, and major organs. These early blueprints are the foundation of what will make your child grow and develop. God's amazing masterpiece is taking form and becoming the uniquely created person He is dreaming of.

Praise God for His works and the creativity of His perfect plan for your child. He has planned and conceived your baby in His supreme wisdom for such a time as this (Psalm 104:24).

Rejoice that your baby is God's workmanship, created in Christ Jesus for good works (Ephesians 2:10).

Meditate on the beauty of God, the master designer/ Like a heavenly artist, His hands are knitting your baby together perfectly at this very moment (Psalm 119:73; 139:13).

Momma,

Your eye color, your bone structure, and the mere shape of your little toe were all created according to God's design. Every detail of you, His daughter, is perfect and precious. You were not cookie-cut from a mold. Imagine His joy in the creation of you. In fact, He had fun making you. How does that change the way you look in the mirror?

# day 30 omnipotent

Have you ever wondered why God would begin forming the brain first and foremost? Today, it is called a "primitive knot," but soon it will become the headquarters for all the other functions of the body. The brain has a supreme role in every major bodily system. Spiritually, Jesus is the creative divine mind behind everything on earth. Praise God for every invention, work of art, and advancement in technology He has downloaded to humanity through thoughts and dreams. Pray that your child's mind will be filled with the amazing mind of Christ.

Pray that God fills your child's mind with skill and excellence to accomplish His will (Exodus 35:35).

Ask God to give your child a mind and heart to work heartily in whatever He calls them to do (Colossians 3:23).

Thank the Lord that your child is God's handiwork, created in Christ to do good works (Ephesians 2:10).

Momma,

You may have had a fleeting fear of bringing a child into this chaotic, dark world. Confess your apprehensive heart to Him. He is sovereign over all, even evil. He uses sovereignty for one purpose: His powerful glory. His "light shines in the darkness, and the darkness has not overcome it" (John 1:5). Praise God today by singing "This Little Light of Mine."

This little light of mine, I'm gonna let it shine! (x3)
Let it shine, let it shine, let it shine!

day 31 — distinct

Today, the building blocks or cells of your baby's development are becoming more distinct. Just as the brain cells differ from the heart cells, so is your little one unique in the assignment God has given him or her. Begin to bless your baby, and wait in hopeful expectation for the good plans your Father already has for them.

Your son or daughter is God's "workmanship, created in Christ Jesus for good works, which God prepared beforehand, that [they] should walk in them" (Ephesians 2:10).

Ask Jesus to let the light within your child shine over the world so others "may see [their] good works and give glory to [their] Father who is in heaven" (Matthew 5:16).

Momma,

You carry within you special gifts and talents that were made to bless and build up the body. Do you operate in the Spirit accordingly? You don't just have a need for the body; the body of Jesus Christ needs the unique, Spirit-manifesting gifts you have. Seek Him today to be filled with His Spirit, so you can fulfill His work on the earth.

rest

You may be wondering why you are so tired. You may even suspect pregnancy is the reason, if you don't yet know you are pregnant. Your fatigue is due to all the hormonal changes going on in your body. While physically you need to rest when you can, spiritual rest is actually a mark of Jesus in your life. Resting in Christ is produced as you trust Him. It comes naturally from a place of intimacy with Him, and spiritual rest is also a key to healing.

Ask God to teach you about His perpetual, never-ceasing rest. He died so that you might enter into His rest and stop striving in your relationship with Him (Hebrews 4:1).

If you've grown weary waiting on a promise to be fulfilled, pray that God will renew your strength. Ask Him to help you continue to do good, knowing you will reap in due season if you do not give up (Galatians 6:9).

Momma,

There is nothing more exhausting than a mind working and thinking nonstop. Fretting, anxiety, and worry all stem from a spirit of fear, rooted in a loss of control. You, beloved, were not made for carrying these yokes. God tells you what to do: Cast "all your anxieties on him, because he cares for you" (1 Peter 5:7). As you know, His perfect love goes deeper and deeper; He promises the outcome will be that fear itself will be banished from your life. What can't you overcome with His peace guarding you? Nothing.

day 33   constant

Along with fatigue, you may already be experiencing nausea. Not all women have the queasies, but if you do, you can talk with your doctor about various treatment options, either natural or medicinal. Nausea and fatigue are actually signs something is now changing within your body. Change can be joyous, not something to be dreaded or feared. Remember, God is constant during the changes and seasons of life.

Praise Jesus, who "is the same yesterday today and forever" (Hebrews 13:8). He is the God who is not driven by circumstances, so thank Him for His consistent, patient love in your life.

God declared, "I the LORD do not change" (Malachi 3:6). He is absolutely secure in Himself, and He is making you into His perfect image (2 Corinthians 3:18). Pray the Spirit will cause you to submit fully and freely to His way in your life.

Numbers 23:19 says "God is not man, that he should lie, or a son of man, that he should change his mind." Ask for deeper and purer faith to trust Him as He leads you daily. He is so pleased with your confidence in Him as you walk by faith and not by sight (Hebrews 11:6; 2 Corinthians 5:7).

Momma,

Today, write your personal prayers and thoughts to the Father in your journal.

day 34   grow

The earliest, tiniest forms of your baby's skeletal and muscular systems are developing. You will grow more amazed at the sheer complexity of this precious one forming within you. Your faith will also grow as you experience God's love and see His attention to every detail of your child's formation. His grand design is always and ever growth with Him. He loves to see His children stretch and mature in their faith too.

Pray your child will grow in grace and knowledge of the Lord (2 Peter 3:18).

Ask that your son or daughter will "grow up in every way into him who is the head, into Christ" (Ephesians 4:15).

Even today, your baby is being transformed from glory to glory, being fashioned in the beautiful image of Jesus (2 Corinthians 3:18). Praise God that there is no season when His glory does not abound.

Momma,

Find an area in your heart where the glory of God may be veiled. Look at the weakness, and thank God that where your self-reliance has ruled, His perfect strength will begin to prevail. The Spirit operates through our humble dependence because He is your eager Helper (John 14:26). Praise Him that He is bringing you to the end of your own power.

day 35   covered

Your baby's blood is already proving vital because it is the forerunner for their newly forming heart and cardiovascular system. How amazing that God's perfect design was for the heart to be created early in the body's development since it will be the source of life for all bodily functions. As you think and pray for your baby's heart, pray for the spiritual heart of your child to be strong, established in truth, and surrendered to the Spirit.

Pray that your child will guard their heart and see it as the place from which flow the springs of life (Proverbs 4:23).

Ask for wisdom as you lead your son or daughter, teaching them not to conform to the pattern of this world. Pray that they will transform and renew their mind, testing and proving God's perfect will (Romans 12:2).

Momma,

Placing your hand over your heart, simply pray Psalm 51:10: "Create in me a clean heart, O God, and renew a right spirit within me."

Thank Him for His cleansing blood and how powerfully it washes away all your unrighteousness. Commit your heart to Him afresh, trusting Him to sustain you against all

Sweet Pea

WEEK

six

day 36   heart

Congrats, Momma, on a milestone—your baby's heart has made its first beats. The complexity of your little one's heart can be summed up in one main job: pumping blood to the brain, lungs, and other organs so they will have the oxygen needed for life. The heart is truly the center of every function in the body. As you think on this, ask how the Father's heart will be manifested on earth through your child.

Pray that out of God's glorious riches, He will strengthen your son or daughter with power through the Spirit in their inner being, so that Christ may dwell in their heart by faith (Ephesians 3:16).

Pray, believing that your child will not let love and faithfulness forsake them and that these fruits will be evident in their lives (Proverbs 3:3).

Momma,

The Father says you are a brand-new creation and that what He has made in you is unlike anything the world has ever seen. What of His heart do you manifest? His love? His joy? You are a living glory carrier everywhere you go. So, how does that change a simple trip to the grocery store? Go, sister. The world needs to see Him in you.

day 37   behold

Look at the calendar again and marvel that after only three weeks, your baby's eyes and ears are forming. Both hearing and sight are unique and special, yet not necessary for life. Think about the gift of sight or the privilege of hearing. As you thank God for these blessings, consider the ability to see and hear in the Spirit. Experiencing His works does not happen naturally, but as He anoints.

Pray that your child will have spiritual eyes to see and spiritual ears to hear.

Write your prayers around the verse "Blessed are your eyes, for they see, and your ears, for they hear" (Matthew 13:16).

Momma,

When was the last time you glanced at heaven and looked fully into the captivating eyes of Jesus? He says of you, His bride,

You are beautiful as Tirzah, my love,

lovely as Jerusalem,

awesome as an army with banners.

Turn away your eyes from me,

for they overwhelm me (Song of Soloman 6:4–5).

Your vision will become His as you behold Him.

day 38   whole

This week, you will want to consider finding a doctor or practitioner who specializes in obstetrics. This is important, not only to check the development of your growing baby but also to ensure you are progressing healthily too. Praise God for so many advancements in healthcare in this era. While medicine can be limited, your Father calls Himself Healer, and He has no limitations. As you pray for your child, thank God for being the healer of the mind, body, and spirit.

Pray and ask the Lord if there is an area of your life He desires to heal, whether physical or emotional. Pray this scripture over yourself as you receive His revelation: "Heal me, O Lord, and I shall be healed; save me, and I shall be saved, for you are my praise" (Jeremiah 17:14).

Ask that "all may go well with you and that you may be in good health, as it goes well with your soul" (3 John 1:2).

Momma,

Healing comes through a total renewal according to the Word of God and what He says over you, beloved. Nothing—depression, disease, nor oppression of any kind—can stand against the revealed Word. Jesus declared on the cross, "It is finished (paid in full)." Do you know the full reward and reality that He gives you as His child? He is offering you healing. Do you trust Him for it, or have you depended on yourself for what only He can do?

humble

A baby at this age is hardly discernible as human; they look like a tiny tadpole in this young season of development. In the weeks and months to come, as God fashions them, they start to become recognizable as a precious human life. In the same way spiritually, there may be parts of your life in an infantile stage that have not fully matured. Don't be discouraged; the Lord makes all things beautiful in His time (Ecclesiastes 3:11).

Ask the Father to show you what His kingdom manifesting in your life looks like (Luke 13:18–21). Pray He gives you vision as you hide His Word in your heart (Psalm 119:11).

Thank Him for small beginnings. Pray for satisfaction and contentment in Him alone, regardless of your circumstances. Praise Him for advancing His kingdom through you and through the life of your child.

Momma,

God delights in taking small, ordinary things and empowering them to showcase His glory. If He can take a few pebbles and slay a giant (1 Samuel 17:1–50), what can His Spirit living in you overcome on a daily basis? You, beloved, are more than a conqueror (Romans 8:37). Go slay spiritual giants in Jesus's name.

day 40   abide

Today, the very first sections of the nervous system are already in place; the spinal cord and brain are also being formed. Your baby's central nervous system is the headquarters for all sensory information, from smell to the smallest movements of muscle. The brain and nerves work in tandem as a team. Spiritually, we know that Jesus is our Head and we are His body. We, as His children, cooperate with His Spirit to go where He says go and speak what He says to speak.

Ask the Spirit to give you His eyes and vision, so you will do only what you see the Father doing (John 5:19).

Pray to abide in His life, dwelling in and drawing from the vine life of Jesus (John 15).

Ask for the heart of Ruth—one of enduring faithfulness: "Where you go I will go" (Ruth 1:16).

Momma,

Ponder your relationship with Jesus. Do you move at the impulses of His love? Do you offer Him excuses and hesitation in your immediate obedience to His leading? If His love wells up in your heart, praise Him for His grace and mercy, thanking Him for making you free to fully obey Him.

day 41 gift

You may start to wonder why your period is late or why certain smells seem stronger lately. These are just a couple of many symptoms indicating pregnancy. Surprise! And congratulations. You have just discovered the wonderful gift of carrying a child, and you will soon discover the blessings of motherhood.

Rejoice in the Lord for this beautiful child, the fruit of your womb a reward (Psalm 127:3).

Know that "out of the mouth of babies and infants" (your child), God has "established strength because of their foes, to still the enemy and the avenger" (Psalm 8:2).

Ask for purer faith to trust God in His promise to teach your child and give them great peace (Isaiah 54:13).

Momma,

You may be excited or a little overwhelmed at the thought of being responsible for the physical and emotional needs of another human being, but God will give you His empowering grace to raise this little one. Trust that as you come to Him with childlike faith, He will take the duty of parenthood and make it a delight (Matthew 18:2).

day 42   expression

If you could peek inside your womb today, you would see a little face forming that has emerging little eyes, nostrils, and an itty-bitty mouth. The face serves an important role in recognition and identity. Your little one will develop and mature, but no matter how much he or she grows, their face will preserve their own distinct look. As you dream of what your child will look like, pray that as they grow in Christ, your son or daughter will become a one-of-a-kind expression of God on the earth.

Thank the Father that your child is predestined for adoption to become a spiritual son or daughter through Jesus (Ephesians 1:5).

Praise God for the new creation your child will become in Christ, not to be compared to anyone else (2 Corinthians 5:17). He or she is a beautiful, unique masterpiece made to reflect the glory of God (2 Corinthians 3:18).

Momma,

When you look in the mirror, are you overcome with the reality that you are a daughter of God? Your Abba, your Daddy, sees the loveliest and most precious face of His Son in you, and you in His Son's. Lock eyes with Him today and you will become everything you see.

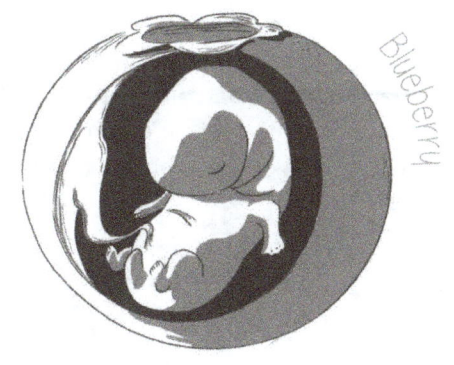

Blueberry

WEEK

seven

day 43 focus

When babies are only about a half-inch long, they develop a lens on each eyeball. This specialized part of the eye allows them to focus light, much like the lens of a camera. Pray that as your child grows spiritually, they will focus on the light of the Father's will.

Pray that your son or daughter will give thanks in all circumstances, for this is God's will in Jesus for them (1 Thessalonians 5:18).

Thank Jesus, the great Shepherd, who will equip your son or daughter with everything good to do His will (Hebrews 13:20-21).

Pray for God's kingdom to come and His will be done in the life of your child (Matthew 6:10).

Momma,

The Lord's will has often been described as mysterious, but a different perspective would be to discover that He delights in your seeking Him, one divine clue at a time. Beloved, He is not reluctant to show you Himself at all. He loves to use everyday things like music, nature, and people to reveal His goodness. Look for Him, and He promises to be found (Jeremiah 29:13). Focus your vision and zoom in on Him. Where did you find Him unexpectedly today?

day 44   protected

The eyes and ears are settling in their permanent place at the front of your child's head. These eye and ear gates are important for receiving or taking in information, but they also need to be protected. Today, as you pray, ask that Jesus will stand guard over the spiritual eyes and ears of your little one, sealing any breach where the enemy might find a foothold in their life.

Pray the spiritual eyes of your child will be healthy, causing the whole body to be full of light (Matthew 6:22).

Ask God to turn the eyes of your son or daughter from looking at worthless things (Psalm 119:37).

Thank your Father, "who is able to keep [your child] from stumbling and will present [them] blameless before the presence of his glory with great joy" (Jude 1:24).

Momma,

Place your hand on your eyes and ask God afresh for His vision—His eyes—to see what He sees. Repent, beloved, if you let the gate of your vision swing wide open to behold anything unholy. As He renews your vision, jot down what you see.

day 45   nourish

Today, your baby is still attached to the sac, but they will soon start being nourished through the vital umbilical cord. This cord will serve as the lifeline between you and your baby. It will carry oxygen and nutrients to feed your little one. As you think of the significance of this membrane, rejoice in how perfectly Jesus serves as the lifeline between you and the Father.

Jesus is the one mediator between you and God. He is the only way to salvation (1 Timothy 2:5). Praise Him for sacrificing Himself on the cross so you and your child could become true children of God.

Pray that your son or daughter will nourish themself on the Word of God (Matthew 4:4).

Just like Jesus multiplied food and fed thousands, pray that He would multiply His provision in your child's life for every season.

Pray that your child will abide in Jesus, the Vine, staying connected to His life-giving Spirit at all times (John 15).

Momma,

As the umbilical cord will be the conduit of nutrition for your growing baby, the Word of God will be the food for your spirit. Beloved, feed on Him daily, hourly—as often as He draws you. You know how essential food is to the body to keep it healthy and full of energy. How much more do you need to eat from the feast of God's wisdom and love to keep your heart and mind healthy? Stay hungry for Him and you will always be satisfied.

day 46

held

Today, your baby's hands are beginning to take shape. They are only tiny buds for the moment, but soon fingers will emerge. The hand is one of God's tools for communication; it writes, constructs, creates, and can be held. Pray your little ones will use their hands for God's glory.

Pray your son or daughter will lift holy hands to bless the Lord (Psalm 134:2).

Ask that God will establish the work of your child's hands (Psalm 90:17).

Rejoice that the Father will strengthen your child and uphold them by His righteous right hand (Isaiah 41:10).

Momma,

The Father says, "I have engraved you on the palms of my hands" (Isaiah 49:16). He holds you (and baby) securely and permanently in His hands. You cannot be un-etched or removed, ever. What an awesome reality that you are forever His child. Because He holds you, He holds all things that concern you. How do you see your circumstances, knowing that His grip secures them? Take heart, sister. His hands hold the whole universe, and He is able to hold your world too.

day 47   wisdom

Your baby's liver will begin working by the end of the week. This special organ serves as the body's ultimate filter, getting rid of waste and toxins from your baby's body. How perfect that God made provision to eliminate what isn't needed, so the body can keep clean from the inside out. As you thank Him for the liver, consider how the Holy Spirit serves as the filter in your heart, helping you discern between good and evil.

Pray for Spirit-filled wisdom for your son or daughter. Ask that God will give your child wisdom from above, which "is first pure, then peaceable, gentle, open to reason, full of mercy and good fruits, impartial and sincere" (James 3:17).

Pray that your child will mature and be able to test every spirit and hold fast to what is good (1 Thessalonians 5:21).

Momma,

Can you imagine trying to raise this baby apart from God's promise of wisdom? The world has wisdom, too, and God describes it as "earthly, unspiritual, demonic" (James 3:15). You will be able to discern between worldly and godly wisdom as you hide God's Word in your heart and walk in step with His Spirit. He gently guides and teaches you, moment by moment, how to respond in His love. You will discover much about wisdom from heaven as you ask in faith. Your Father promises to give it to you lavishly, never shaming you. Tell him what you need wisdom for.

mind

Your baby's body is small compared to its developing head. This is important as the head is the headquarters for the nervous system and the senses, like sight and hearing. Your baby's brain will develop rapidly during this embryonic period. You can begin to imagine how careful you will be with your little one's delicate head once she or he is born. When they learn to ride a bike, you will make sure they wear a helmet.

Pray that along with the ability to think and reason, your child will walk with the mind of Christ Himself (1 Corinthians 2:16).

Pray that your son or daughter will not be conformed to the world but will be transformed by the renewing of their mind (Romans 12:2).

Ask that God would prepare the mind of your son or daughter for action, being sober-minded, setting their hope fully on the grace that will be brought to them at the revelation of Jesus (1 Peter 1:13).

God tells us clearly what to think about; pray that your child's mind will be controlled by love, thinking on whatever is true, honorable, just, pure, lovely, commendable, excellent, and worthy of praise (Philippians 4:8).

Momma,

"As he thinks in his heart, so is he" (Proverbs 23:7 NKJV). Jot down the last five thoughts you've had. They don't have to be significant or earthshattering, but were they set and surrounded in truth? Did they well up anxiety or rest? Your beautiful Jesus invites you to take on the reality of thinking the way He does—with a heavenly vantage point. He gives you Himself, the Living Word of God, and offers what the world could never give: abundant life. Abide in Him and let His words abide in you (John 15:7). Your mind will be renewed, and you will manifest the wisdom from above (James 3:17).

day 49 foundation

Your baby's foot has now appeared at the end of the leg bud, although it is not fully complete with toes yet. Feet are a wonderful part of God's design; they steady the body and will give your child the ability to stand, walk, or run. The foot is quite literally the foundation of the body. The Father has purposed the feet to carry the rest of the body. As your feet go, so you go. Pray that your child's steps will be established in the Lord.

Thank God for bringing strength to your child, making their "feet like the feet of deer," and setting them on His high places (Psalm 18:33).

Praise Him for preparing the feet of your son or daughter with the gospel of peace (Ephesians 6:15). He describes their feet as "beautiful," as they carry the good news to the lost (Romans 10:15).

Psalm 119:105 says, "Your Word is a lamp to my feet and a light to my path." Ask that God's Word would illuminate the steps of your child as they walk in truth.

Momma,

Every place your foot treads has already been given to you in the Lord (Joshua 1:3). How does that change the way you view the mundane, everyday errands you make, like trips to the grocery store? Your steps are perfectly ordered. "The steps of a man are established by the LORD, when he delights in his way" (Psalm 37:23). You have divine permission to take ground for the kingdom, one step at a time. Spend time asking Him today where He dreams of taking you.

Raspberry

WEEK

eight

day 50   lifted

Your tiny little one is barely the size of a pencil eraser, yet their arm bud has already developed an elbow. Their arms will lengthen and form hands with fingers soon. But the elbow, while often overlooked unless hit (ouch!), has been purposed by God for extending, reaching, and giving your arm the ability to bend. Life would be a challenge if you could not bend your arm. Today, thank God that He has already made provision for your child to lift their arms in praise to Him.

Praise the Lord, who has done wonderful things. "His right hand and his holy arm have worked salvation for [your child]" (Psalm 98:1).

Thank God for His love over your child. He declares, "Even to your old age I am he, and to gray hairs I will carry you" (Isaiah 46:4).

See the heart of Jesus when "he took [the children] in his arms and blessed them, laying his hands on them" (Mark 10:16). Ask Him to lay hands on your baby and bless them. What did He bless them with?

Momma,

When your little one is born, it won't be long until he or she learns to reach for you, seeking comfort. It's innate and God-inspired to cry, arms held out, ready to receive love. He is so willing to hold you close in His arms as you extend yours to Him. Reach up, literally, saying, "Abba, I need You. Hold me." He will cup you in His lap as you feel the strength in His arms. Your heart will be established and your heart's cry will diminish. Your soul will soon be like a weaned child's, calm and content (Psalm 131:2). His presence has surrounded you in love, and you will learn His rest.

day 51   grace

Today, as your little one's brain, heart, and skeleton develop further, you may be feeling nauseous, better known as morning sickness. This queasy feeling can leave you tired and running for the bathroom. It can be triggered by certain smells and foods, and it's most likely caused by changes in your hormones. Take heart, sister; it can possibly be a good sign that your placenta is growing normally, although every woman's pregnancy is unique. Worshipping can be a key to overcoming challenges in the next few weeks. Continue to praise God for this new life, trusting Him to be your strength when you feel weak.

"'[My] power is being perfected [and is completed and shows itself most effectively] in [your] weakness.' ... the power of Christ [may completely enfold me and] may dwell in me. ... for when I am weak [in human strength], then I am strong [truly able, truly powerful, truly drawing from God's strength]" (2 Corinthians 12:9-10 AMP).

Pray that when your son or daughter encounters a time of weakness, they will be able to rest in the empowering grace of God. Ask that your child rejoice in and draw from the joy of the Lord being their strength (Nehemiah 8:10).

Momma,

There is much power in resolve. When you have purposed and determined in your heart that you will praise God in all circumstances, a new strength rises up from within the deepest part of you. This is the strength of Jesus that proclaims, "I can do all things through Christ" (Philippians 4:13). His grace will enable you right now to walk through difficulty—morning sickness, relational turmoil, or anything—with confidence that He is willing to bear the fruit of love, joy, and peace in you and through you.

day 52 spoken

Your little one is growing rapidly, with all their minute parts forming and being knit together. Their lips are beginning to separate from the nostrils and form a distinct place of their own. The lips are perfectly designed to move as they take in food and air. Your child's soft lips are also important for speaking. Of all the words your child will say, the ones declaring who they are in Christ will be the most important. Ask the Father to give your child boldness and faith to speak His gospel, sing His praises, and declare His truth.

Pray that the Lord will set a guard over your son or daughter's mouth and keep watch over the door to their lips (Psalm 141:3).

Ask that your child will continually offer up sacrifices of praise to God—"the fruit of lips that acknowledge his name" (Hebrews 13:15).

Thank God for His faithfulness to cleanse and forgive your child as they confess their sins (1 John 1:9).

Momma,

What do you want to say to your Father today? Just as you sit and dream about what your child's voice will be like, so He sits and longs to hear you talk to Him. He loves your presence as much as you adore His. He created you for relationship with Him, which includes all aspects of affection: sharing, laughing, listening. Whatever is on your heart, know that you, daughter, can come boldly before the throne of grace and find mercy for every need (Hebrews 4:16).

day 53   balance

Your baby's ears are noticeable now and soon will move into their permanent place on the sides of your child's head. Each ear will form a pinna, or outer ear, with its typical funnel shape. How amazing that God perfectly designed this shape so it can best navigate sound into the ear. The ears are also important for balance. This intricate organ contains tiny amounts of fluid and sensors that maintain balance for the rest of the body. Spiritually, your child will need balance in the Lord to not be weighed down by the things of the world.

Pray that your son or daughter will learn to be content in all circumstances (Philippians 4:11).

Declare your child will seek the kingdom of God and His righteousness, knowing that all other things will be added to them (Matthew 6:33).

Pray the Lord will teach your child to serve from a pure heart, knowing that "many who are first will be last, and the last first" (Matthew 19:30).

Ask that God will cause your child to "lay aside every weight, and sin which clings so closely, and let [them] run with endurance the race that is set before [them]" (Hebrews 12:1).

Momma,

Soon your life will create room for a whole new balance. You will adjust time and rearrange priorities based on the need. But God is the best organizer and planner. Begin now to live with a schedule submitted to Him. You will be amazed at how it multiplies time and productivity simply because you trusted His ways above your own. He is the author of balance and order, and He is making you just like Him.

day 54   expression

Your little one has been growing for just over a month, and already their brain is working. Exactly what your little one is pondering, no one knows except the Lord. Soon, however, their facial expressions will let you know exactly what's on their mind. The muscles in their face will curve into that precious smile or into a frown. The face is a true mirror for the condition of the heart. Pray that your son or daughter will express grace always from a heart filled with God's love.

The Lord promises that when your child looks to Him, they will be radiant and their face shall never be ashamed (Psalm 34:5).

Your son or daughter will become beautiful as they spend time beholding the Lord. Let their heart's cry be, "Let me see Your face, let me hear Your voice, for Your voice is sweet, and Your face is lovely" (Song of Solomon 2:14).

Ask the Lord to give your child a happy heart. "A glad heart makes a cheerful face, but by sorrow of heart the spirit is crushed" (Proverbs 15:13).

Momma,

Some sisters vibrantly demonstrate what's going on in their hearts, the proverbial "wearing their heart on their sleeves." Others, not so much. It can be hard to tell from their countenance if there's an internal battle being waged. But God knows it all. He is the God who looks at the heart, not the external appearance (1 Samuel 16:7). Today, take comfort and refuge in your Father, who knows you better than you know yourself. Look deep into His eyes. Don't glance. Learn to behold Him and you, too, will become a living expression of His beauty.

day 55   covered

Your little one has already formed nerves, which will soon enable them to move on their own. While your baby continues to grow, your blood volume will almost double during the next six weeks to sustain the pregnancy. The extra blood won't necessarily be noticeable, except for some weight gain, and your heart is working a little harder. In the spirit realm, the blood of Jesus has wonder-working power when you apply it to your child's life.

Pray that your son or daughter will be purified by the blood of Jesus, which empowers them to have confidence to enter the Holy Place (Hebrews 10:19).

Thank God that He made a way for your child to have peace and reconciliation with Him through His blood being shed on a cross (Colossians 1:20).

Your son or daughter is so precious to Jesus that He bought them with His own blood (Acts 20:28). Spend time praising Him for His incredible sacrifice and love.

Momma,

There is nothing more impenetrable than the blood of Jesus. What can touch its power and not be forever changed? Where His blood is applied and appropriated, there is cleansing, healing, and forgiveness. Write down your prayer of gratitude that He has covered you in the fount that never runs dry.

day 56 position

Your baby has been curled in a crescent shape for weeks, but soon that tiny body will stretch out and change position. As their legs and arms lengthen, their body uncurls and can move more freely. The timing of your child's life is perfect on the Father's kingdom calendar. Their position in the kingdom is completely dependent on having life in Christ. Their position in time will never change in Christ, but their posture will change with different seasons. Pray that your son or daughter will learn to live from heaven to earth.

Ephesians 2:6 says He "raised us up with him and seated us with him in the heavenly places in Christ Jesus, so that in the coming ages he might show the immeasurable riches of his grace in kindness toward us in Christ Jesus."

Pray that once cognitive, your son or daughter will ask the Lord for heavenly perspective, always setting their mind "on things that are above, not on things that are on earth" (Colossians 3:2).

Ask the Father to give your son or daughter a posture of prayer and thanks in all circumstances (1 Thessalonians 5:16–18).

Momma,

You have a wonderful advantage in Christ: the ability to see from above. Since you're seated in heavenly places, you can ask the Father to show you what He sees for your life. You can rise above circumstantial living (always being up or down, dependent on the moment). Today, you can begin living with a beautiful view, soaring high above like an eagle. This way of perceiving takes time and practice, but the Holy Spirit will not leave you until it is accomplished. Doesn't that sound like freedom?

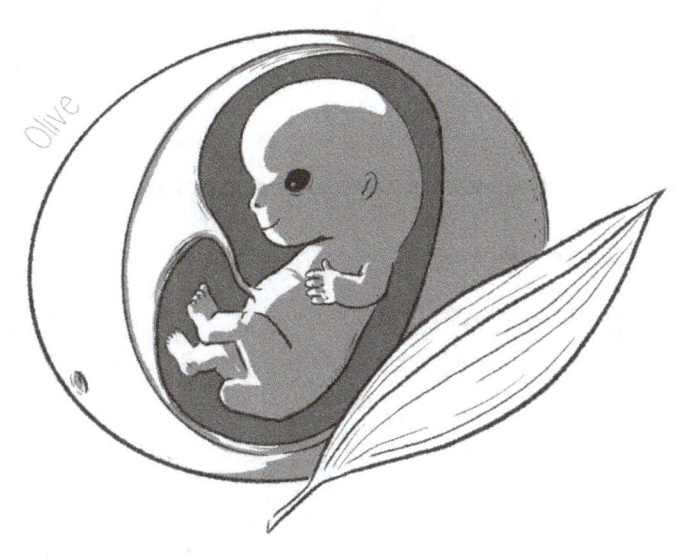

Olive

WEEK

nine

day 57　harmony

Today, your baby has already developed their thyroid gland, which is complex and incredibly important for every hormone in the body. The thyroid regulates body temperature and ensures that all the organs are operating in perfect unison. What a fascinating feat at only forty-three days old. God designed all the parts of the natural body to work together in harmony, and He also made a way for the spiritual body, the church, to operate as one.

Pray that your child will love the bride of Christ, always praying for and maintaining unity in the Spirit. Pray for your son or daughter to be perfectly united in mind and thought with other believers (1 Corinthians 1:10).

Ask that God would give your child a heart like His, bearing with believers, forgiving them, and putting on love, which binds everything together in perfect unity (Colossians 3:13–14).

Ask the Father to give your little one a heart of humility (Romans 12:16).

Momma,

Your place in the body of Christ is specific and unique. You are a one-of-a-kind creation of God. Your growth in the Lord and with His bride will flow from cooperating with the Spirit with your gifts. You have been given gifts in the Spirit; when joined together with other members, they will cause growth for not only you but for everyone. The whole body will build itself up in love (Ephesians 4:16). Imagine a symphony of instruments and the beautiful music it creates. Jesus is the conductor, orchestrating a heavenly sound throughout the earth when we play our part.

healer

Your little one's flexible cartilage is beginning the transition to bone, which is denser and harder. It's God's blueprint for the bones to harden so the whole body can be supported. One area, however, that is not intended to ossify or harden is the heart. Your little one's physical heart is fleshy and full of blood-pumping life; likewise, the inner self, or the heart, must remain free from hardness and bitterness to stay healthy. A hardened heart can stop the flow of the Spirit. Pray that your son or daughter will walk in humble forgiveness, not letting their heart become hardened by relationships or trials.

Pray your child will have ears to hear the Spirit and not harden their heart to His voice (Hebrews 3:7).

Ask the Lord to give your son or daughter a humble, repentant heart so they will not be hardened by the deceitfulness of sin (Hebrews 3:13).

Pray your child will not harden their heart toward their neighbors nor love them in word only. Pray they will open their hearts to give as the Lord leads (1 John 3:17).

Momma,

A bruised and hardened heart needs to be handled tenderly. The Lord promises that a "bruised reed He will not break, and a smoldering wick he will not quench" (Matthew 12:20). Jesus's strength is coupled with the fruit of gentleness. He doesn't just possess gentle qualities but is Himself gentleness. He is a gentle man. You can freely bring Him the parts of your heart where bitterness hides. He will whisper His love right into that broken place. And just like a wilted flower finds new life after being watered, so the Son will shower you in His Spirit. You will come to know Him as more than Savior. You will begin to call Him your healer.

day 59 servant

Today, your little one is free to move around your womb with lots of sudden jolting. These movements are too small for you to notice, and they are just muscles responding to signals from their spinal cord. It's funny to imagine all this going on inside your very own body while you cannot feel anything. This is likened to serving. A humble servant loves for the sake of love alone, as a blessing not to be noticed. Pray that your child will serve others with their life, desiring to take last place so others can be lifted up.

Pray that your child will have the mind of Christ (Philippians 2:1-8).

Ask God to give your child a heart to wash the feet of others, both literally and through acts of kindness.

Thank the Holy Spirit, who will give your son or daughter opportunities to grow in humility (1 Peter 5:5). He will give them eyes to serve others, and they will do so graciously and without grumbling.

Momma,

*Can anything be more servant-like than being a mother? Soon your plate will be full, tending to your baby with sides of extra laundry and dishes. Maybe the term "serve" feels negative to you. The Lord simply wants **you**. Your only service to Him is love. He does not need you to do things for Him but rather be with Him. He will do the serving in and through you. It will be joyful and willful rather than dutiful. He will cause the most mundane chores of life to be adventures where He meets you with experiences of His love. Doesn't that sound fun?*

day 60   speak

You have probably already had your first prenatal appointment to see how your little one is growing. You will hear the tiny heartbeat and see precious pictures on an ultrasound. You are just getting accustomed to the news that you're having a baby. Your doctor has confirmed your child's estimated birthdate. What you speak concerning this little one is vital. God says, "Death and life are in the power of the tongue, and those who love it will eat its fruits" (Proverbs 18:21). Your words have that much power. There is great authority in blessing your child. You don't have to wait until you see them. Practice blessing your little one now.

Speak directly to your baby; this is different from praying for him or her.

If you know a name you will potentially use, speak it aloud. Talk to your baby as if he or she can understand now, and when your little one arrives, blessing will be their natural language. Express how desired they are by you and God. This is the antidote to rejection. For example, you may say something like this: "You are a dearly loved child of God. You have been blessed in Christ with every spiritual blessing in the heavenly places" (Ephesians 1:3). Other blessing scriptures include Psalm 127:3-5; 139:13-16; Proverbs 1:8-9; Jeremiah 1:5; and Ephesians 2:10.

Momma,

You may have grown up being wanted by your mother, or you may have felt rejection. The awesome reality is that your heart can be free today regardless of what was passed on by your parents. Confess your desire to forgive your parents if the language spoken over you was hurtful or negative. Your soul can be restored back to love and acceptance. Ask the Holy Spirit if there's any area of your soul that was wounded from birth by either your mother or father. His beautiful grace is enough to cover every word and bring healing today.

unity

As your baby continues to develop, you may be preparing for your little one to be welcomed by a sibling or two. While having multiple children brings a new level of responsibility, you will also see your love multiply. Mommies can often fret that their love will diminish for one child in favor of another, but God created you in His image, and He loves all His children uniquely. Begin to ask God for grace and love to fill the hearts of older siblings. They might need a little encouragement in the transition, but you have an endless supply of the Father's goodness. He loves to cover everyone under the eternal umbrella of His love.

Pray that your children will have hearts full of brotherly love toward one another, outdoing each other in honor (Romans 12:10).

Psalm 133:1 says, "Behold, how good and pleasant it is when brothers dwell in unity." Praise God for the way He brings unity and peace to the siblings in your household.

Ask the Father for a spirit of forgiveness for your children, so they will walk in Him, immediately releasing offense when it occurs.

Momma,

As your heart has been set on grace and forgiveness for your child, turn to your own heart. Ask the Holy Spirit to search it. Confess the love you have for your own siblings as well as your spiritual siblings in Christ. Thank God for His love and how He loves others through you. Pray blessings specifically over those who have wounded you. Remember the power of your tongue, the spoken word. It flows from your heart. Thank Him for purifying your heart and words today.

day 62   stretch

Today, in addition to morning sickness, you may also experience aches from your womb being stretched to accommodate your growing baby. These sharp pains in your lower abdomen are normal; the ligaments and muscles are being stretched, just as you will be stretched spiritually. Growth and stretching are normal parts of your spiritual life. Don't despise the pain. It's often in that place that God will manifest Himself mightily to you. Truths you believed in your head will become real in your heart.

If something painful has touched your life, find comfort in His Word, especially from the psalms.

Psalm 34:18 says, "The LORD is near to the brokenhearted and saves the crushed in spirit." Thank Him for being close to you in the midst of your trials. He will never leave you. Thank Him that when the pain is intense, His love will overshadow you.

Psalm 23 is profoundly comforting. Ask Jesus, your Shepherd, to refresh your weary soul. Thank Him that His goodness and love will follow you all your days.

Thank Him that He "comforts us in all our affliction" (2 Corinthians 1:4). The Father of compassion is your comforter. Set your mind on His faithfulness and identification with earthly pain.

Momma,

Pain is inevitable. Jesus actually promised you will have it, but it was never meant to define you (John 16:33). Shadrach, Meshach, and Abednego were not remembered for going into the fire but for coming out of it untouched (Daniel 3:26–27). Jesus wants to accomplish the same unbinding in your heart. He has purposed fire to show you His glory.

day 63   miracle

Your seven-week-old baby is only slightly bigger than an almond and already has a heartbeat reaching 150 beats per minute. What a miracle! Also, the Master Craftsman has designed your little one to respond to touch already. It is a sheer wonder that such a small human with a functioning brain and heart is growing inside you. What other miracle do you want to see manifest in your life? Be assured God is still the God of miracles. He can open deaf ears, raise the dead, part whole seas, and bring water from a rock.

Trust His Word because the Lord declares that nothing is too hard for Him (Jeremiah 32:27).

Ask Him for faith to believe. He declares that "all things are possible for one who believes" (Mark 9:23).

Consider what you are asking of God. Maybe it's too small. He makes an astounding promise in Ephesians 3:20 that He "is able to do far more abundantly than all that we ask or think, according to the power at work within us."

Jot down the miracle you need in the notebook you have set aside for thoughts and prayers during your pregnancy.

Momma,

God's miracles were always attached to His love. He performed the miraculous to show not just His greatness but also His great love. He performed signs and wonders throughout time to tell His children, "See? I can take care of you like no other. Trust Me." He can provide for your biggest financial, physical, and emotional needs. He knows you better than you know yourself. Confess His love over your life (Psalm 63:3), and watch your faith for miracles begin to emerge.

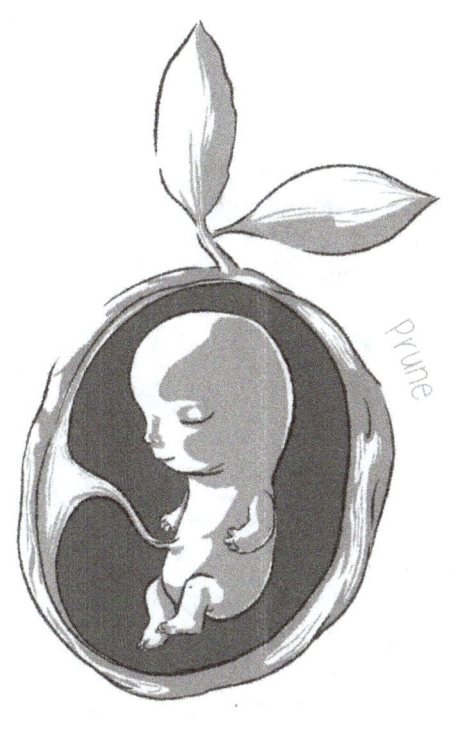

prune

WEEK

ten

day 64   time

You are entering your eighth week of pregnancy and your bump is starting to emerge. You will experience many seasons with this child, such as toddlerhood and the teenage years, and they are designed for dependence and intimacy with God. Spiritual seasons can last days, months, or years, and you cannot hurry them. They are intended to work in you what the Father wills, and they are always, always for your good.

Thank God for the season you're in currently. Thank Him for His purposes being worked into your heart as you learn to trust Him minute by minute, hour by hour (Ecclesiastes 3:1).

Rejoice that He is right now working all things together for your baby's good because you love Him and are called according to His purpose (Romans 8:28).

Praise Him that He promises you will reap in due season if you don't quit (Galatians 6:9). Ask Him for Spirit-filled endurance and patience (Colossians 1:11).

Momma,

Stop and think about the natural season you're in at the moment. Is it winter—barren and cold outside? Or it is spring, when you're seeing all the signs of new life budding from the ground? Your circumstances, even the difficult ones, are perfecting something of Jesus in your character. He uses the good and the bad to conform you to Himself so He will be expressed through your life more and more. Rejoice. Take heart. He is not wasting a thing in your season. You don't have to delay the joy until this season passes. He wants to show you the beauty of this day, this trial, this winter, or this wilderness. And the beauty is always Him.

day 65

fixed

Your baby is growing rapidly and changing shape daily. Today, their forehead is the most pronounced feature on their body. Oh, to think of all the kisses that will be placed on that precious spot. The forehead is often overlooked, but it serves as part of your child's appearance. What lies beneath his or her forehead is spiritually significant: the mind. It's one of the biggest targets of the enemy, but God has given His promise that your child can have the mind of Christ, thinking His thoughts and overcoming any natural reasoning. Your child's mind can be filled with the spirit of life (Romans 8:6).

Ask God to impress His Word on the heart and mind of your child. Ask Him to give you a heart to teach them to love His Word (Deuteronomy 11:18-19).

Thank Him that your child will set their mind like flint to follow and love the Lord (Deuteronomy 6:4-9).

Pray that the spirit of your little one's mind will be renewed by the Word (Romans 12:2).

Ask God to give your child views of heaven and set their mind always on things above (Colossians 3:2).

Momma,

Set your mind on heaven. Ask, "What does heaven have for me?" and listen or see with your mind to experience the glory of heaven's treasures and receive gifts and answers to your questions. Why else would your Father tell you to set your mind there? He says you are seated in heaven (Ephesians 2:6), and Jesus tells you to ask for the Father's will to be done on earth "as it is in heaven" (Matthew 6:10). How can you bring heaven to earth if you can't communicate with it? Write down your experience.

Your baby has every organ in place; each one continues to grow and mature. And within just two months in your womb, your child is starting to move their tiny limbs distinctly. What do you imagine when you think of your little one moving their arms? Or stretching their legs? It's exciting to think that one day your child will be on the go, crawling, walking, running. God has designed the body to progress from those baby steps to a fully mature person able to move in a million ways.

Pray for the destiny God has for your child. As they grow, ask for glimpses of the way your child will "live and move and have [their] being" in Christ (Acts 17:28).

Pray that the heart of your child will grow in wisdom as you impart the Word to them (2 Timothy 3:14-15).

Just like Jesus grew, ask the Father to increase your little one's wisdom and stature and their favor with both Him and other people (Luke 2:52).

Pray your son or daughter will speak truth and grow up in every way into Jesus, the Head of the body (Ephesians 4:15-16).

Momma,

As your baby is growing (literally), let that be a reminder of the need to grow in faith and wisdom. You've asked for wisdom for your child, now ask for yourself. God makes an amazing promise: If you need wisdom, He will lavish it on you with no shame (James 1:5). There should never be a time you say, "I don't know what to do." That wells up hopelessness and powerlessness. But your Father simply wants you to ask for wisdom. He will pour out His thoughts and mind concerning you. What a gift that is, but it's so rarely accessed. He is waiting on you to ask, so go ahead.

day 67   fragrance

The olfactory neurons, responsible for your baby's sense of smell, have formed and matured. What an often-overlooked gift the sense of smell is. Your child's ability to smell can be a delight when you give them special treats like brownies. Smells can also warn of danger if you sniff smoke from a nearby fire. As you thank God today for the blessing of this sense, consider the spiritual fragrance of your child. Pray that your son or daughter will carry the beautiful fragrance of Christ everywhere they go.

Pray that your little one will walk with the aroma of Christ (2 Corinthians 2:15).

Ask that they will walk in love, just "as Christ loved us and gave Himself up for us, a fragrant offering and sacrifice to God" (Ephesians 5:2).

Momma,

The idea of being a soothing aroma emits pleasant thoughts of peace. Think about the fragrance of freshly cut gardenia or hyacinth blooms. Your presence in any room, beloved, can be pleasant or stinky. Have you ever considered that? The Holy Spirit in you is the perfume of Christ to some, leading to life. His aroma may cause another to turn his head in disgust, leading to death. It is a putrid smell that offends their heart. The smell, of course, is spiritual. The longer you linger in His presence, the more you will take on His nature and fragrance.

day 68   tender

Your baby's brain is developing, along with the surrounding skull. Because their head will continue to grow in size, God designed your little one with a soft spot, a fontanelle. Of course, the bones will eventually fuse, causing the fontanelle to close. While your baby has a soft spot on their head, pray that their heart will remain soft as well. Having a tender heart is key to receiving from the Lord. Your child's relationship with both the Lord and the body of Christ depends on their heart being soft in the Spirit.

Ask God to show your son or daughter His kindness and forgiveness so they will be tenderhearted, kind, and forgiving toward others (Ephesians 4:32).

Pray that they humble themselves before the Lord and maintain a contrite heart (Psalm 51:17).

Ask the Father to give your child soft answers that turn away wrath (Proverbs 15:1).

Pray for your son or daughter to have "unity of mind, sympathy, brotherly love, a tender heart, and a humble mind" (1 Peter 3:8).

Momma,

Your heart is like a sponge: if it's never engaged with the river of living water, it will become dry and hard, unusable. But once the Spirit seeps into the fibers of your heart, it will become soft, pliable, and able to be fully used. The next time you do dishes, stop and pray. Ask the Spirit to wash over your heart, softening the hardened or dry areas. Thank Him for awakening a thirst in you for Him.

day 69   faith

Today, your baby is very close to three months old, and your little one is only about 1.5 inches long. Their little eyes are closed, with the eyelids being fully formed. The eyelids will stay fused until they reach twenty-four weeks. Just as the eyes will remain shut, pray that as your child grows, they will walk by faith, not by sight (2 Corinthians 5:7). Faith isn't blind but rather the assurance of things you cannot see (Hebrews 11:1). Faith is the only way to please the Father. Pray for the faith of your son or daughter to be rooted deeply in the love of God.

Pray that faith will be imparted and established as your child listens to God's Word and hears the voice of the Spirit. This isn't merely hearing with physical ears but hearing with spiritual ears (Romans 10:17).

Ask that your child have faith to believe that whatever they ask God for in prayer, they will receive. Thank the Father that He is going to give your son or daughter the ability to perform mighty acts through faith (Mark 11:22-24).

Pray that your child's faith does not rest on the wisdom of men but in the power of God (1 Corinthians. 2:5).

Momma,

You are closer than you think. The faith to believe God isn't hard to achieve. In fact, it's a gift that was given to you freely (Ephesians 2:8). You didn't ask for it. Anytime you call on the Father, it's because the Spirit has drawn you to Him. You can try to love Him, worship Him, and spend time with Him apart from faith. But when faith from His heart is added to love, worship, and intimacy, true transformation happens. Nothing changes without faith. It's the only way to please God because true faith is based on relational trust (Hebrews 11:6). He is your Father. You're His beloved daughter. What can't He do for one of His own children?

day 70   knit

Your little one has a very immature but functioning digestive system in place. A process called peristalsis in your baby's large intestine helps relax and contract the muscle to push food through for digestion. In the same way, God uses food for fuel in our bodies, often without our acknowledgment. The daily relaxing and contracting of your baby's intestine is God's design. He is often working and orchestrating complex circumstances unbeknownst to us. Pray that your child will be aware of the Father's glory all around him.

Pray that as your child grows, they will find awe and wonder in God's creation. May they see His glory in flowers, the planets, people, and everything He crafted (Psalm 19).

Bless your child with the realities found in Romans 8:28-29, which says God's glory can be found in all circumstances as your child loves Him.

Pray God's glory will manifest in your child's life as His power works infinitely above anything for which they could ask or imagine (Ephesians 3:20-21).

Momma,

You may be peeping in the mirror a little more frequently these days, ever checking your tummy to see how you're growing. A perfect promise is given to you in 2 Corinthians 3:18: "And we, who with unveiled faces all reflect the Lord's glory, are being transformed into his likeness with ever-increasing glory." Your reflection in the mirror is more than what the eye can see; you are projecting to the world God's glory. As you grow in faith, you are growing in Jesus's image of love, grace, and hope. And you look beautiful, beloved.

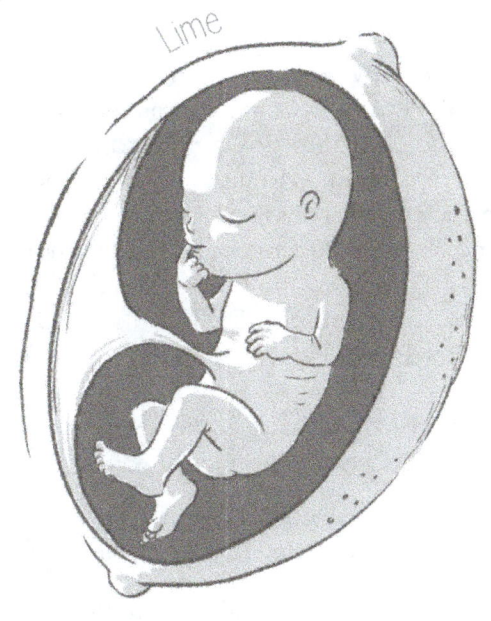

Lime

WEEK

eleven

new

At this stage, your baby has made some pretty exceptional strides in growth. Today, they have become complete in every way, except for maturation. All major organs are in place and functioning. Their lips, eyes, and toes are present. And if you were to peek inside, you would notice that something was missing: the tail. No longer visible, the tail is gone, leaving the familiar form of a tiny human body. Spiritually, as your child comes to know the Lord, the old will pass away, making way for the new (2 Corinthians 5:17). Praise God today for the way He makes all things new (Revelation 21:5) in your little one's life.

Pray that your son or daughter will be filled with the new wine of the Spirit and become a living wineskin (Matthew 9:17).

Ask the Spirit to empower your child to walk in newness of life, to raise them from spiritual death, as Christ was (Romans 6:4).

Praise God that He has appointed and declared salvation over your child, causing them to become a brand-new creature (2 Corinthians 5:17). Your child will become someone incomparable and completely unique, unlike anyone else on earth.

Pray that your little one continually presses on and keeps their eyes on the prize of Jesus, not looking to the past (Philippians 3:13).

Momma,

What does "new" feel like to you? Maybe it brings to mind the New Year's ball dropping, signaling a fresh start on life. Maybe it feels like getting a new pair of comfy shoes or even something simple, like that first cup of fresh coffee in the morning. There's something about the new, unused, and unspoiled parts of our life that we love. Ridding ourselves of the old can be difficult because those once-new things have become so comfortable. But your Father is always about the new. He is not satisfied with refurbishing the old. He declares that He makes "all things new." What part of your heart has He made new, yet you're hanging on to the old?

day 72 generation

Soon you will mark yet another milestone, Momma. You will begin your second trimester. With this new beginning, consider the significance of this baby. This little one marks the beginning of another generation, possibly making you an infinite great-grandmother one day. How faithful is God to you and the generation to come. Today, with the leading of the Spirit, write down a blessing over your family line from here until eternity. Blessing is different to prayer in that you are speaking God's heart over people, invoking blessing for well-being, prosperity, and protection. Study the patriarchs of the Old Testament like Abraham and Isaac, who spoke unalterable blessings over their sons.

Father, may you bless my generation to come with

_____.

By the blood of Jesus, thank You for graciously and thoroughly cleansing my generation from _____.

I praise you, God, for the promises You have made to my family (Isaiah 44:3-5; 54:13; 59:21; Psalm 112:1-2; Proverbs 14:26). You are faithful forever and ever.

Momma,

You are a source of blessing for your child and your family. Never forget that God has made you exactly the way He has so you can be a blessing to others. Just by existing, you are a blessing!

> "The LORD said to Abram, "Go from your country and your kindred and your father's house to the land that I will show you. And I will make of you a great nation, and I will bless you and make your name great, so that you will be a blessing. ... and in you all the families of the earth shall be blessed."
> —Genesis 12:1-3

day 73   led

Today, your little one is secure in your womb. Over the last several weeks, you have prayed over many details of your son or daughter. You've asked the Father to pour out His blessing over both the physical and spiritual parts of your child. One of the greatest joys in life is learning to be led by the voice of the Spirit. As you pray today, ask Him what details He wants to speak to you. Sit in His presence. Worship Him. Listen for His leading.

Pray that your little one will be led by the Spirit, so they will quickly choose to be adopted into God's family (Romans 8:14).

Pray for the Holy Spirit to intercede for you, your husband, and your child(ren) according to the will of God (Romans 8:26-27).

Ask God to reveal things to you about your baby (1 Corinthians 2:7-11).

Ask that your child be always led by the Spirit instead of the law (Galatians 5:18).

Momma,

The Father delights in childlike questions such as, "What do You want to say about my child?" Write down His answer. The Father often likes to speak in clues, only giving part of a whole. He may speak one word or give you a phrase, a scripture, or an image in your mind. These are all various ways the Spirit can reveal Himself. Ask Him what He is saying to you. Very likely you will know through the interpretation of the Spirit without having to ask. But should you desire to know more, ask. Trust Him if He doesn't answer immediately. Listening and being led by the Spirit is a lifelong process of learning to trust His love. And it is always an adventure.

hidden

Your baby's gender was determined earlier, at conception. Right now, their gender is still a secret in the heavenlies because your little one has no outward genitalia. The sex will be revealed within the next few weeks, and you will discover whether your bundle of joy is a baby boy or girl. Your all-knowing Father in heaven has many secrets He wants to share with your child (Matthew 13:11). Pray that your son or daughter will seek Him in the secret place, waiting on the Lord to manifest His will on earth.

Pray that your child will dwell in the secret place of the Most High and "abide in the shadow of the Almighty" (Psalm 91:1).

Ask God to grant your little one a desire to pray and seek intimacy with the Lord at a young age (Psalm 36:7). Know that as they draw near to the Lord, He will draw near to them (James 4:8).

Thank the Father that He will be a hiding place for your child, surrounding them with deliverance from the enemy (Psalm 32:7).

Momma,

Imagine a place where you go to meet with the Lord. It's just you two. You share the deepest longings of your heart there. You sit at His feet, pouring out affection only for Him. His presence fills that sacred place as you declare the wonder of His love. You declare your praise to Him as He declares His praise over you. He wants to be with you as much as you want to be with Him. He is found in this place, the secret place. His Spirit is drawing you there today. He says, "Call to me and I will answer you, and will tell you great and hidden things that you have not known" (Jeremiah 33:3).

day 75 unmistakable

The fingerprints are not yet formed on your baby's fingertips, yet their fingers will grip around very tiny objects placed in their hand. Fingerprints are an unmistakable mark of identity. With their special design, our fingerprints help identify exactly who we are to the world. As your little one matures, so will the rest of their body, but their fingerprints will remain unchanged. As you're thinking about the magnificence of God's creative design, pray that your child's identity will be found in Christ alone.

Pray your son or daughter will be found in Christ and become a brand-new creation (2 Corinthians 5:17).

Ask the Lord to reveal to your child that they are "his workmanship, created in Christ Jesus for good works" (Ephesians 2:10).

Pray that your child does not walk in condemnation but trusts Jesus's death on the cross as the finished payment for their sins (Romans 8:1).

Momma,

Your identity and security are completely in Jesus. Be reminded today how immensely and lavishly loved you are by your Father. Isaiah 43:1 tells you that God calls you by name, and you are His. You are precious in His sight, honored, and loved. Think of how much you love your child already. That love will continue to grow and grow, but God's love does not grow. It's constant and perfect, not needing to be perfected or increased. It's full and complete. And so are you, in Him.

pure

Your baby's genitalia are developing into a male or female shape. The hormone testosterone will determine if your baby has a penis. If none is present, you will have a baby girl. The Lord has known long before this day His plan for giving you a son or daughter. Pray that God will keep him or her pure in body, mind, and soul. As these sexual organs are forming, ask for your child to maintain sexual purity after puberty and for the rest of their life.

Pray that your child's body will be used only for the Lord, not given to any immorality (1 Corinthians 6:13).

Ask the Lord to give your child understanding at a young age that their body is a temple of the Holy Spirit and does not belong to themself (1 Corinthians 6:19).

Pray that your child will know how to "possess his own vessel," or have self-control "in holiness and honor, not in the passion of lust" (1 Thessalonians 4:4-5).

Momma,

As you prayed today for your son or daughter's purity, you may be pondering your own decisions regarding sex. Your thoughts may have turned to shame over past sexual sin, or maybe you delighted in waiting until marriage to have sex. Beloved, if you made decisions that were not God's will for your life, He is offering you grace and forgiveness. His love covers a multitude of sins, and He promises to take even the guilt away (Psalm 32:5). The Father delights in saying, "Let me clean you, and you will be whiter than snow" (Psalm 51:6-7).

 connection

Your baby's cranial nerves, which cause the eyes to move, are developing at a rapid rate. Their eyes' ability to see is totally dependent on the nerves connected to their brain. Without their brain, sight would not be possible. As you pray for these connections to be strong and healthy, ask God to give your child a spiritual connection to the body of Christ that is established in love.

Pray that your son or daughter will have an understanding of the body of Christ having many members, yet being one. Pray that they will love the body of Christ (1 Corinthians 12:12-14).

Ask that your child be eager to maintain unity in the Spirit (within the body of Christ) and keep the bond of peace (Ephesians 4:2-3).

Ask Him to give your little one sincere love for their spiritual brothers and sisters—a fervent love from the heart (1 Peter 1:22).

Momma,

You are connected, whether you feel like it or not. When you were born again into the Father's family, you were woven beautifully into the family of faith and gained many spiritual siblings. The blood of Christ makes this possible. Thank Him for the way He specially gifted you in the Spirit to build up and edify the body of Christ. You were born into a kingdom that cannot be shaken (Hebrews 12:28). Where do you see His glory shining most in the body of Christ?

WEEK

twelve

day 78

stand

The parts of your baby's brain responsible for coordination and balance are making connections with the rest of the body. Their spinal cord is also developing. One day, your tiny baby will mature into a toddler, standing on their own two feet. The ability to balance is an amazing aspect of God's design.

When you pray, think about the heart of your child, asking God to cause your son or daughter to stand firm in their faith (1 Corinthians 16:13).

Pray that your child will stand in awe of the Lord and praise Him (Psalm 22:23).

Pray the full armor of God over your little one (Ephesians 6:11). As you pray, trust that God will establish your child so they can stand against the schemes of the devil.

Momma,

Your emotional ability to coordinate and balance will become strengthened by God's grace when you are finally able to bring your baby home after birth. Your Father doesn't have a perfect-momma checklist, but He delights in perfecting mommas. So, turn your expectations from yourself to Him. Let His Spirit show you hour by hour the power of His promises.

day 79   seasons

Your baby's spinal cord "tail" at the base of their bottom is reducing in size and will disappear well before birth. Even as your adult body grows and changes, your child, too, will have not only significant changes in their body but in their spiritual development as well. What God teaches your child in one season of their faith will give way to another season of growth in Him. As they mature, old, fleshly mindsets disappear, being replaced with truth and freedom in Christ.

Pray that as your child grows, they will be like a tree planted by streams of water that yields its fruit in its season and whose leaf does not wither (Psalm 1:3).

Ask God to show your child how the whole of life is rooted in His rhythms and that "for everything there is a season," according to Ecclesiastes 3:1-8. Pray He guards their heart from being wrapped around earthly affections and they would choose to always set their eyes on Him in each station of their life.

Thank God for the grace of disappearing mindsets! He will upgrade your child's thinking to be transformed to His with each milestone (Romans 12:2).

Momma,

The many seasons of your life will produce a particular fruit according to that season. Just like in natural seasons—for instance, berries are harvested in summer and cabbage is produced in the winter—you can expect that God is perfectly bearing out the fruit of His Spirit at any particular time in you. All the fruit is grounded in the soil of His love. Bring your heart before God and ask Him to water those fruits with the Holy Spirit, so that others may be nourished by Him in you.

day 80 foundation

Your baby's tiny body is taking shape amazingly. Their little spinal vertebrae in the upper chest cavity and neck are beginning to harden. Their neck provides a stable foundation for their head. Myriad nerves and vertebrae in the spinal cord establish control over the movement of the rest of the body.

Pray your child will not become stiff-necked or obstinate before the Lord but will live in complete surrender that comes from love (Exodus 32:9).

Ask the Lord to change the heart of your son or daughter so that they desire obedience and turn from any stubbornness in their spirit (Deuteronomy 10:16).

Pray that the Father would be gracious and merciful, just as He was to Israel when He daily stretched out His hand of blessing, despite their disobedience and contrariness (Romans 10:21).

Momma,

Pride is the ultimate cause of our sin. We believe we can reason better, provide better, even parent better than our all-wise Father. Confess any area of your heart where you sense you have been stiff-necked. It may manifest with thoughts like, **I'm not changing. I won't do that unless _____ happens.** *Your Father loves to be gracious (Isaiah 30:18) and teach you a better way: love. Surrender everything because of His great love for you. You will soon see His way is not just a better way but the only way.*

day 87   pure

Your baby's kidneys have begun to function, producing urine, which is excreted into your amniotic fluid. The kidneys help keep your body healthy and clean. It is impossible to survive without at least one functioning kidney. Pray for your child that just as their kidneys work to remove waste, they will walk in regular repentance, keeping their soul clean before the Lord.

Praise God because when your child repents, heaven rejoices (Luke 15:10).

Pray that when your child sins, they will have "godly grief [that] produces a repentance that leads to salvation" (2 Corinthians 7:10).

Pray that God, Himself, will grant your son or daughter repentance, leading them to a knowledge of the truth (2 Timothy 2:25).

Momma,

Let the Spirit search your heart today. Have you come to the end of yourself, your will, your thoughts, and your default reactions? Because you are God's child, you have already been washed with the blood of Jesus. The goal of repenting is not to get rid of sin; that was accomplished on the cross. The goal of repenting is to become one with Jesus, one in thought and heart. If the Holy Spirit shows you something, thank Him for making you freer. You will come to know that repentance is such a gift.

day 82   feast

Your baby's jaw is complete with tiny tooth buds, while the buds for
the permanent teeth are situated near the inside of their baby teeth.
Your little one's ability to chew will take many months to mature. The
teeth are important for chewing, and they aid in swallowing and
even digestion. When you consider everything your son or daughter
will develop a taste for, pray they will chew or feast on the promises
and truths of God's Word.

Pray that your child understands that they do "not live by
bread alone, but by every word that comes from the mouth
of God," His living Word (Matthew 4:4).

Pray that they will listen to the Lord, eat what is good, and
delight in the abundance of God (Isaiah 55:2).

Ask God to give your child a great love for Jesus, that they
would eat the living Word as they partake of the Lord's
Supper regularly (Matthew 26:26).

Momma,

*You may feel like you're eating everything, or the opposite may
be true; the thought of food may be repulsive. While you can
physically reach the point of fullness or overeating, this concept
isn't true of the Bread of Life, Jesus (John 6:35). Your intake of
His presence and Word can never be exhausted. His kingdom
provides a never-ending banquet of love, joy, peace, and
wisdom. Bon appétit.*

day 83 discern

Your baby can now react to differing degrees of temperature—either cold or hot. Their skin's sensitivity to touch is maturing in a very specific pattern. The skin is our largest organ and can be a lighthouse that signals danger to the body. It can be burned by the sun or any hot element, as well as be damaged by exposure to extreme cold. As you pray over your child's reactions, consider the spiritual side of their responses.

Pray that just as their skin is sensitive, their heart will be sensitive to the Spirit, discerning and responding to all things in love.

Pray that your son or daughter's love will grow more and more in all knowledge and discernment (Philippians 1:9).

Ask God to give your child His wisdom, knowing that He promises to give it generously and without shame (James 1:5).

Momma,

You want to be the best momma. Being a great parent comes from being loved by the best Parent. Spend time with God, getting to know His voice and tone. He will teach you His patient love. He will be gracious to you when you deserve to be grounded. He will extend mercy and kindness to you when you are at your worst. And He longs for you to be just like Him, beloved.

voice

Your little one's larynx or voice box is developing, but she or he can't make any sounds quite yet because your fluid-filled womb does not have access to air. Your son or daughter's very first cry will indicate they indeed have their own distinct little voice. Their voice may be shrill at times, like when they are crying to be fed, but at other times, their soft coo will reveal their contentment. As you think about their voice, pray that your child will listen to and obey the voice of the Lord.

Praise the Lord that He hears your child's voice as they call to him in prayer (Psalm 5:3).

Pray that your child will give ear to the gentle nudging of the Spirit, listening to and obeying the words of God (Isaiah 28:23).

Ask the Spirit to give assurance of His voice to your child, so your child will follow Him everywhere He leads (John 10:27).

Momma,

Jesus makes you this promise: If you ask, you will receive (Matthew 7:7). He further promises that you do not have because you do not ask (James 4:2). How amazing that God says there are things in your life you could have based only on one condition: asking. Get ready, your child will one day be asking you lots. They will ask for toys, for treats, for your time, and for help. You will soon discover how much joy it is to give them what they seek. Obviously, you won't give them everything, but you will bless them as you see fit. Your Father loves to give to you. What do you need or want today?

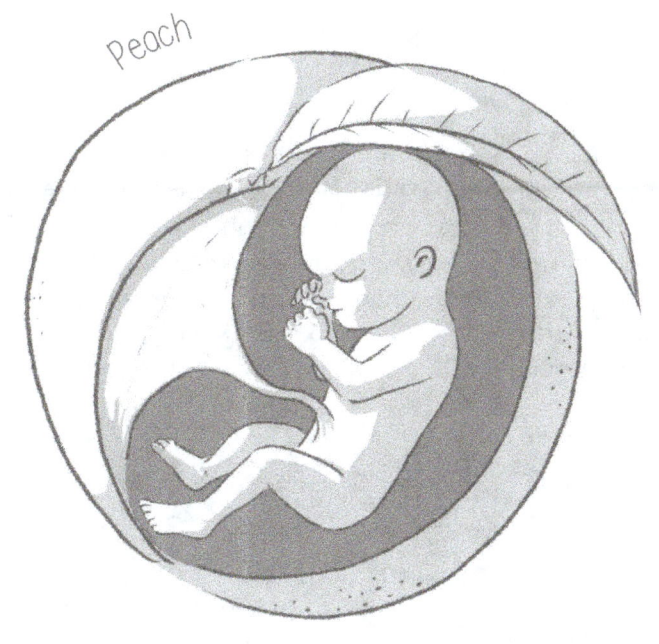

Peach

WEEK

thirteen

day 85 increase

Your pre-pregnancy uterus has doubled in size to make room for your growing baby. The uterus is your baby's home for the next eight months; it will continue to stretch and grow perfectly proportionately to your baby's size. With this idea of your uterus expanding, pray today that as your child matures in the things of the Spirit, God will powerfully allow them to see the kingdom expand and increase through their life.

Ask the Lord for a love of the kingdom of God to come fully into the heart of your child (Matthew 6:10).

Pray the Lord will advance His kingdom through the prayers and witness of your child (Matthew 13:31-33).

Ask that God will draw your little one close and will cause them to know Him as their "Holy One, the Creator of Israel, [their] King" (Isaiah 43:15).

Momma,

You are a princess, a royal daughter of the King of all Kings. He rules in peace and sees all things with a wise perspective. He is not viewing your circumstances with one fretful, anxious thought, so, beloved, why are you? Let His love usher you into His royal courts. Come before your King of Peace, grab a hold of His throne, and find in Him everything you need. That is the law of His land: you have full and free access to this approachable King. How does that drive out a mindset of lack?

day 86

secure

Your baby's internal organs will soon be protected by their ribcage, which is made of hardened bone. These bones protect all the soft organs, like the heart and lungs. Without their ribs, your baby's major organs could not withstand a traumatic injury. As you pray for your child's physical protection, rejoice in the spiritual protection God gives. He is the guardian of your son or daughter's soul.

Ask the Lord, who is faithful, to strengthen and protect your child from the enemy (2 Thessalonians 3:3).

Thank God for being your child's refuge and protection in the midst of trials and storms (Isaiah 4:6).

Pray your child will fully rely on the Lord's protection when they feel threatened, allowing the Spirit's peace to flood their heart (Isaiah 27:5).

Momma,

Just as your ribcage guards your internal organs, so should you guard your heart. Allow the Holy Spirit to examine your deepest thoughts. Don't be afraid to see what still remains there. It's going to be exposed to the beautiful light of His truth, then completely uprooted. Allow your Father to shower His grace on you. Feel the freedom of that exchange: your ashes for His beauty.

day 87   rest

Believe it or not, your little one can yawn now. The exact purpose and function of the yawn is not fully understood, but for sure, it can be a sign of tiredness. The body needs rest daily. God designed you for rest, and even spiritually, He designed your soul for rest in Him. In fact, rest comes from faith.

Pray that your child will rest soundly in their body. Ask that they also rest spiritually in the finished work of Jesus's death and resurrection.

Pray that your child will wait on the Lord, gaining new strength. Ask that they run with Him and not grow tired (Isaiah 40:31).

Praise God that He does not become weary or tired. Thank Him for sustaining you (Isaiah 40:28).

Pray that your little one will not grow weary in doing good (Galatians 6:9).

Ask for their rest to be found in Christ alone and that your child will cease working for God and instead simply abide in Him (Matthew 11:28).

Momma,

T.I.R.E.D.
Volumes can be written on the weariness that accompanies motherhood. You have many nights of interrupted sleep, often after taking care of cooking, cleaning, and possibly caring for your other children. The awesome news is that the Holy Spirit is called "the Helper." And He can never be exhausted. You cannot weary Him with your cries for help. He is never too tired to listen or too busy to answer. His supply of strength is endless and vibrant. Is your body telling you to rest? Or maybe your mind needs to be fixed on the Word, renewed from anxiety. Come, snuggle up in Abba's lap.

day 88   strength

The muscle movements of your baby have become more intentional and coordinated. They seem to be moving their tiny arms and hands purposefully now. They may even put a hand in their mouth simply because they are curious. Amazingly, these movements will grow stronger and more choreographed. Ask the Lord today to give your child the revelation of their purpose for being and living.

Thank God for His good plans for your child, plans that are for their well-being and for their future (Jeremiah 29:11).

Pray that your little one will perceive the good works God has prepared and called them to walk in and do them (Ephesians 2:10).

Ask that your child will reflect the light as they do good works, causing many to glorify the Father (Matthew 5:16).

Momma,

Though it may seem your entire purpose for living will change with the arrival of your baby, it actually won't change. You becoming a mom only highlights your relationship with your Father. Your time may be consumed with your baby, but your heart can remain in adoration and worship of God. Ask that you will have an undivided heart as you become a momma, staying in your true purpose of being a much-loved daughter. That's why you were made: to be loved and to love the One who made you.

day 89   taste

Your baby's ability to taste is in place. Their little taste buds are mature and concentrated on the tongue now. Think of their first small tastes of milk and baby food. Soon they will have their own preferences for what veggies and fruits they like. Their tastes will grow, and eventually, they will settle on the foods they like best. As you're considering all the dishes you will serve your little one, pray that their heart will taste and see the goodness of God.

Ask that your child experience and taste the fruit of the Spirit in their life (Galatians 5:22).

Pray that your son or daughter will hunger and thirst for righteousness (Matthew 5:6).

Thank God that He prepares a feasting table in the presence of your child's (spiritual) enemies (Psalm 23:5).

Pray that your little one will share in unity with other believers, partaking of the Bread of Life—Jesus (1 Corinthians 10:17).

Momma,

The Lord invites you to His banqueting table of love. He delights in satisfying your heart, guaranteeing that as you come to Him, you will never be disappointed. He wants to give you a steady diet of love, joy, and peace as you trust Him. You cannot be nourished on vitamins alone. Put away human supplements and people's commentary. Come to the Living Water, the Bread of Life, the One who feeds you Himself. Imagine the health of your spirit as you feast on Him.

day 90   offering

Did you know your baby's sense of smell is now developing? Their olfactory sense, as it is called, can detect different scents, even in your womb. Smells or aromas are significant to the Lord. Incense and spices were offered to Him in the Scriptures, which typically meant sacrifice. Pray that your child will live the sacrificial life of Jesus, so many may be blessed.

Pray your son or daughter will give off the pleasing aroma of a sacrificial love before the Lord (Leviticus 6:15).

Spend time praising Jesus for His great sacrifice, given for the sins of the whole world, including your child's (Hebrews 5:1).

Journal your own prayer of thanks and praise.

Momma,

You're beginning to understand the meaning of sacrifice as a parent. Pregnancy causes you to forgo some of your unhealthy eating and sleeping habits. You give these up for one reason: love. You already love this tiny human enough to put his or her needs before your own. Considering that God doesn't have any needs but is completely driven by His love for you, how does that change the way you understand sacrifice? You're not driven by duty but by delight. In comparison to what Jesus gave, what are you really giving up?

day 97

protect

Your baby's skull has taken shape and is becoming very hard. It is making room for the ever-growing brain. The protection provided by the cranium will prove vital as your little one's brain grows. Just as the brain needs the constant covering of the skull, so your child needs the Lord's faithful protection over their life.

Thank God for protecting your little one wherever they go (Psalm 91:14).

Praise the Lord that He directs mighty ministering angels over your child that will guard them in all their ways (Psalm 91:11).

Thank Him that because He is faithful, He guards your son or daughter against the Evil One (2 Thessalonians 3:3).

Momma,

Your ability to protect your child will be tested. Do not fear. Anything that you and your child will face has already been overcome by Jesus. He is your defender, your protector, your overcomer. If you have been perfected in His love, there's no fear you cannot look squarely in the eye. Fear is paralyzing, but love is freeing. Ask Him to give you faith to trust His love alone for you, your family, and your little one.

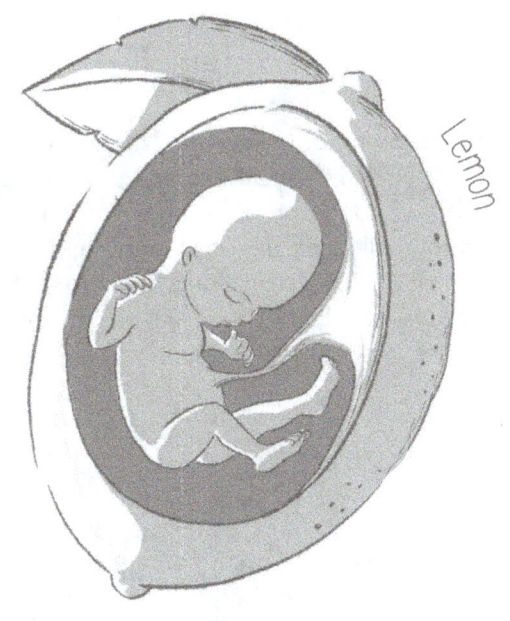

Lemon

WEEK

fourteen

day 92

grace

Your baby's life-giving blood now has the amazing ability to coagulate or clot at this point in their development. This God-designed function helps your baby's body stop excessive bleeding due to injury. One day, your baby will grow into a young child, then on to adulthood, with a variety of relationships along the way. With many relationships, offenses are possible. Pray your child will forgive quickly when he or she experiences an emotional wound.

Pray your child will be kind and compassionate to others, forgiving, just as Christ forgave them (Ephesians 4:32).

Ask God to give your child a heart filled with perpetual forgiveness, not counting offenses against others (Matthew 18:21-22).

Praise God that your child can live in the goodness and forgiveness of Christ, abounding in His constant love (Psalm 86:5).

Momma,

Right now, you cannot imagine your precious baby having conflict in life, but they no doubt will. In their school years, they might have friendships that grow and then suddenly fall apart. You will be tempted to help resolve these relational difficulties yourself, but God will teach them much about His love, grace, and forgiveness as they learn to live like Christ.

day 93

sweet

Amazingly, at just twelve weeks, your baby already prefers sweet tastes over sour ones. Their ability to distinguish between and choose from different tastes will carry well into childhood. Your son or daughter will have many opportunities to allow the Holy Spirit to make them sweet in soul. These trials will be suited specifically for the spiritual growth of your child. You may be tempted to pray the tests away, but allow God's perfect purpose to be worked into your child's heart through them. Pray that in all circumstances, your child will respond in grace, not bitterness.

Pray the sweet words of the Lord will abound in your child (Psalm 119:103).

Pray your little one will use their mouth for building others up, speaking graciously to everyone (Proverbs 16:21; Ephesians 4:29).

Ask the Lord to guard your child from bitter speech, that they would always speak words of life from a pure heart (James 3:11).

Momma,

You have been given authority to speak life over your child. What does that mean? Simply put, when you open your mouth, your words can promote hope and life or destruction and death. The prayers you are sowing into your son or daughter's life are like sweet-smelling incense to God. His heart is tender toward the cries of a mother. Truly, may the meditation of your heart and the words of your mouth be pleasing to the Lord (Psalm 19:14).

Your precious little one is now developing very soft nails on their tiny toes and fingers. The purpose of the fingernails and toenails can often go unnoticed—until you have an itch. The most insignificant details of the body become very important when they're needed. God designed the weaker members of the body to function alongside the stronger ones. Each has its purpose. Spiritually, He chooses the weaker things in the world's eyes to display His glory. Pray that your child will glorify God as they depend on His strength, not their own.

Pray your child will not desire to become wise in their own eyes (1 Corinthians 1:27).

Pray the Spirit will give your son or daughter understanding that when they are weak, God's strength will be perfected in them (1 John 2:5).

Ask for your child to have humility of mind and for them to regard others as more important than themself (Philippians 2:3).

Momma,

Pregnancy is a beautiful gift from God. These nine months are a time for you to trust in the Lord and see Him skillfully knit your baby together. At the appointed time, you will meet your precious baby, looking him or her in the eye, finally seeing the fruit of these prayers. And you may turn your head to the heavens and wonder at the creativity and beauty of God, knowing that He alone created this little miracle you're holding. Spend time praising His faithfulness today.

day 95

hear

Your baby's ability to respond to loud sounds shows great progress in their development. While their response may be delayed by seconds, he or she can feel the soundwaves. They will grow in their reactions to the multitude of sounds they will hear all through childhood. Learning to obey the Lord's voice will be a process, especially as they grow in understanding God's Word. Pray that your son or daughter will be led by the Spirit and quickly say yes in response.

Ask that the Lord would grant your child spiritual ears to hear (Psalm 95:7).

Pray God opens the door of your child's heart, so they can receive sonship (Revelation 3:20).

Pray your child will respond quickly to the direction of the Holy Spirit, not hardening their heart in disobedience (Hebrews 3:7-8).

Momma,

The Lord's voice isn't hard to discern. His voice is truth. He always builds up and speaks in wisdom. He speaks love, even when He is disciplining. There is a rest that always accompanies His presence, while the world speaks the language of busyness, anxiety, and impatience. It demands and never gives while placing burdens and expectations that can never be met. Listen for that still, small voice. Quiet your heart, beloved. Shhh ... what's He saying to you?

day 96

Your baby may now have a response to touch, even showing signs of reacting to being tickled. When you think of playing with your child, you know tickling him or her will produce the sweetest laugh. The memories and moments you will create as you play with your child will be some of the most joyful times in your life. As you think about the fruit of joy, ask that your son or daughter's joy will be found in knowing Jesus.

Ask that the joy of the Lord will be your child's strength (Nehemiah 8:10).

Bless your little one with the true fruit of joy, asking that it not be rooted in circumstances or others (Galatians 5:22).

Pray that your child will count it all joy when they suffer in trials (James 1:2).

Momma,

Jesus is the most joyful person. He brings a lightheartedness and rest to every situation you face. He longs for you to have His joy in all things. When the mundane, everyday tasks of motherhood attempt to veil the joyful moments, be encouraged that Jesus desires to produce more than a feeling in you. Joy naturally flows from faith, not emotion. The beautiful reality is that Jesus becomes your joy. His smile, His love, His affection, His pleasure over you is enough, beloved.

peace

Your little one is already becoming adapted to a noisy world outside the womb. All the gurgles and sounds happening inside their little world right now are quite soothing. Think about the different sounds you hear each day; your child's generation will know the sounds of cell phone rings and technological alerts from a very young age. All of that can create a hurriedness that could rob your child of rest. Pray that your little one will walk in the peace of Christ.

Ask the Father to give your child peace, not as the world gives, but as Jesus promises (John 14:27).

Pray your son or daughter will set their mind on the Spirit, who gives life and peace (Romans 8:6).

Pray that your child will strive for peace with everyone (Hebrews 12:14).

Momma,

Where do you turn for rest? Every heart has a default, an automatic place where it seeks solace. Confess your need **for** *Him, not simply to Him. Allow Him to set the atmosphere of your heart. Do you need His peace to drive out busy and hurried thoughts? Imagine worry being overwhelmed by His love, swallowed up until it completely dissolves into nothing. See all your troubles in the light of His grace and love.*

day 98　strength

If you are having a baby boy, he is now producing the hormone testosterone. The Lord designed our bodies to primarily function through hormones, which control many aspects of our day-to-day operations. The male sex hormone is what gives little boys the ability to mature into men. As you pray today for your son, ask that God will bless him with a revelation of his identity as a son. Knowing who he is as a child of God is the foundation of relating to Him. Pray now for the roots of this understanding to be established in truth.

Pray that your son will be a mighty man of valor in his generation.

Ask that he will fear God and walk in strength (1 Corinthians 16:13).

Pray your son will understand that godly masculinity is grounded in meekness and humility.

Momma,

Your influence in your son's life is significant. Consider the Proverbs, where King Lemuel's mother was giving wise counsel to him (Proverbs 31). The gentleness of the Spirit will manifest as you teach your son; you will display true femininity as you serve and show him how he ought to bless his sisters in Christ. He will come to see all girls as beloved daughters of God and treat them so.

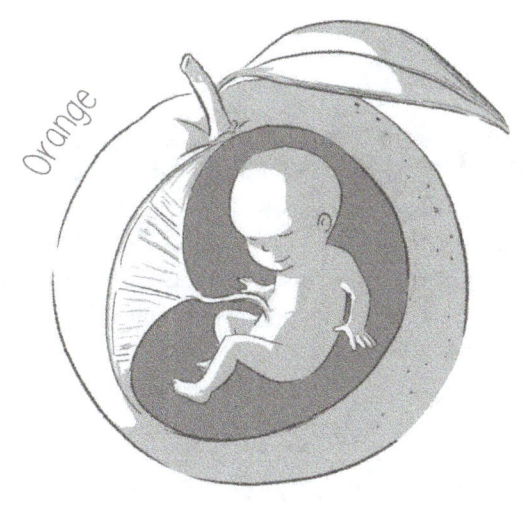

Orange

WEEK

fifteen

day 99 — content

Congratulations! In many ways, the hardest and easiest aspects of pregnancy are complete. Morning sickness is likely subsiding, and your energy level may be picking up. Soon the bump will be showing more, and you will enter the trimester where you will experience those little flutters in your tummy becoming stronger kicks. As you transition from one trimester to another, pray that God will give you contentment in every season.

Ask the Father to teach you the secret of contentment in whatever state you find yourself, whether life is fruitless or flourishing (Philippians 4:4-9).

Pray that you will give thanks in all things (1 Thessalonians 5:18).

Ask for your heart to rejoice always, finding your true source of joy in Jesus, "and the peace of God, which surpasses all understanding, will guard your hearts and your minds in Christ Jesus" (Philippians 4:7).

Momma,

The Lord always has you looking forward to what's ahead. He is leading you along with His love so, you don't have to fear change. Change becomes obsolete when you live, move, and have your being in Christ (Acts 17:28). He is always with you in every season of life. If God calls you to make a major move or career change, you can trust Him. His blessing will follow your obedience; don't wait for faith before you step out. Faith is not blind. It's bedrock trust in your Father. You will see His amazing provisions, which will manifest mainly in your heart. You will experience His peace, His joy, and His empowering grace along the way, and those, beloved, are eternal.

day 100   blessing

Your baby's mouth is maturing, with their tastebuds in place, along with the ability to salivate. Your little one's mouth will be used for more than eating; it will be the source of everything he or she says. What they will say is directly connected to what is in the deep well of their heart. Today, as you're praying for your child's mouth, pray that their speech will be submitted to the Spirit and that it will glorify the Lord.

Pray that your child will use their mouth for blessing, not cursing (James 3:10).

Ask the Father to give your child a heart filled with love that overflows in words that edify and minister grace to all who hear (Ephesians 4:29).

Pray that your son or daughter will confess their sins to the Lord, not harboring anything unrighteous in their heart (Psalm 51).

Momma,

There's great power in the things you speak. You can use your voice to bless or curse, but God says His children should never curse others. He always calls us to speak pure words. He says we are deceived if we bless Him one minute while cursing our brother the next. Saltwater and freshwater cannot flow from the same source. He is your source, beloved. If your words have been less than a blessing, use that same tongue to thank Him for revealing that to you. Thank Him for His forgiveness and goodness to cleanse you and cause you to speak as He speaks: full of wisdom, love, and grace.

day 101   serve

Your baby's hand has formed and matured to look just like yours, only much tinier. Each little finger is distinct and able to wiggle. The hand is an amazing member of the body. Think of the many uses God designed just for the hand: holding, writing, pointing, gripping, and touching. When your baby is born, you will look in wonder at their precious hands. How fun to dream of the ways God will use those hands one day. May the Lord bless your child with holy hands that serve Him and others.

Pray that your child will serve often and humbly and not let their left hand know what their right is doing (Matthew 6:3).

Thank the Father that your child is being knit together by His holy hands. Your son or daughter is clay in the Potter's hands (Jeremiah 18:6).

Pray that your child will lift holy hands in praise to God (1 Timothy 2:8).

Momma,

Those precious, gentle hands of Jesus were pierced for you (Psalm 22:16). If you should ever have a doubt about His love for you, you're not alone. Remember the disciple Thomas, and Jesus's response to his doubts? The Lord invited Him to literally touch the place where He was wounded and believe (John 20:27). Recall the ways Jesus used His hands: to heal, to hold, and to bless. And He is the same today, yesterday, and forever. Those same hands long to touch that place in your heart that needs assurance today.

day 102 grace

Babies can now move very fluidly in the womb, which will be a change from life outside your warm, dark tummy. Soon they will emerge into a world filled with light and different temperatures. They will be able to stretch out completely or love being snuggled tight, depending on their mood. Just as they will have adjustments from one familiar environment to another, ask God to give your child grace and security in every change of life.

Thank the Lord that while life is constantly changing, Jesus never changes. He is the same "yesterday, today, and forever" (Hebrews 13:8).

Ask the Lord to give your child an understanding of His all-sufficient grace for every circumstance (2 Corinthians 12:9).

Pray for peace over your child's mind and that he or she keeps it fixed on the Lord. He promises perfect peace as your child trusts Him (Isaiah 26:3).

Momma,

When something happens in your life that causes tension, you may be tempted to pray it away, when often the Lord will use that very thing to purify your heart and give Him great glory. Remember, your Father is always, always pursuing a relationship with you. Do not resist the changes in life; they are purposed by Him to draw you close. He truly knows what's best for you, beloved. Allow faith to rise up in your heart and mind, trusting in every word He speaks to you.

day 103

Your baby's ribcage and sternum or breastbone is beginning to harden. These bones are significant features as God created a special protection for their most precious organ, the heart. As you are praying for your baby's heart, interceding for him or her will be their greatest protection. Your prayers are the spiritual "ribcage" which will guard your little one's life. Your prayers are precious to the Father.

Thank Jesus, who is ever interceding in heaven for you and your child (Romans 8:34).

Praise the Holy Spirit, who intercedes to the Father when you don't know how to pray (Romans 8:26).

Ask the Lord to empower you in faith as you present your prayers and petitions to Him for everything that concerns you (Philippians 4:6-7).

Momma,

Praying for your child will be one of your greatest "labors" of love. He will use those prayers to reveal His own love to you. You will see that prayer really is just relationship: talking, listening, laughing, crying, and enjoying one another. You will bring your child to Him, just as you are even doing now and calling him or her by name, to the Father. Let His promise wash over your spirit, taking it in with full faith when He says "all your children shall be taught by the LORD, and great shall be the peace of your children" (Isaiah 54:13).

day 104 dependent

Your little one's neck is continuing to grow. The muscles that hold the head are strengthening and will continue to grow after birth. A baby's fragile neck needs lots of support when you hold them, mainly because it is directly connected to the brain. The neck and the brain depend on each other to operate in a healthy way. Today, as you're praying and thinking about your baby's neck, consider how your child will need to live in total dependence on the Lord to stay spiritually healthy.

Ask the Lord to give your son or daughter a submissive heart to the Spirit, and pray they will trust His Word and leading (Psalm 78:1).

Praise God that He alone will sustain your child in every trial in life (Psalm 55:22).

Pray that your child will seek God's kingdom first and know that earthly things will fade (Matthew 6:28-33).

Momma,

Childlike dependence is being worked into your soul through this pregnancy. You are learning to trust your Abba or Daddy, as opposed to yourself. He says, "Apart from me you can do nothing" (John 15:5), but have you tried doing things on your own? You may be able to do lots of things, but He says you will be powerless as you do them. He wants to do life **with** you. Imagine a God who wants to be with you all day, then watch you as you sleep. You are His prize, beloved. Confess your self-will and determination to do things on your own, and trust His grace to provide all you need.

day 105   held

Your baby's sweet little hand is able to show greater signs of grasping. How wonderful is the simple ability to grasp. Consider how frequently your child will hold an object—a sippy cup, a crayon, a toy, and, most importantly, your hand. Think about the spiritual side of grasping—to hold fast to the Lord and not let go. This is the desire of every Jesus-loving parent for their children.

Ask the Lord to manifest humility in your child. Jesus "did not count equality with God a thing to be grasped, but emptied himself, by taking the form of a servant, being born in the likeness of men. And being found in human form, he humbled himself by becoming obedient" (Philippians 2:6-8).

Pray that your little ones will hold fast to their confessions of hope and not doubt (Hebrews 10:23).

Pray that your child will hold on to what is good as the Spirit leads them to examine everything (1 Thessalonians 5:21).

Momma,

God is love (1 John 4:7-8). He declares you are His precious lamb, and He holds you in the palm of His hand. You're secure in Him, a safe place where no one can snatch you from Him (John 10:29). Praise God that His love will never let you go, and nothing and no one will ever separate you from Him (Romans 8:38-39). You may know that in your head and agree. But, beloved, when that reality grips your heart, you will find new joy and purpose for life. Let the truth reassure you of who you really are—His.

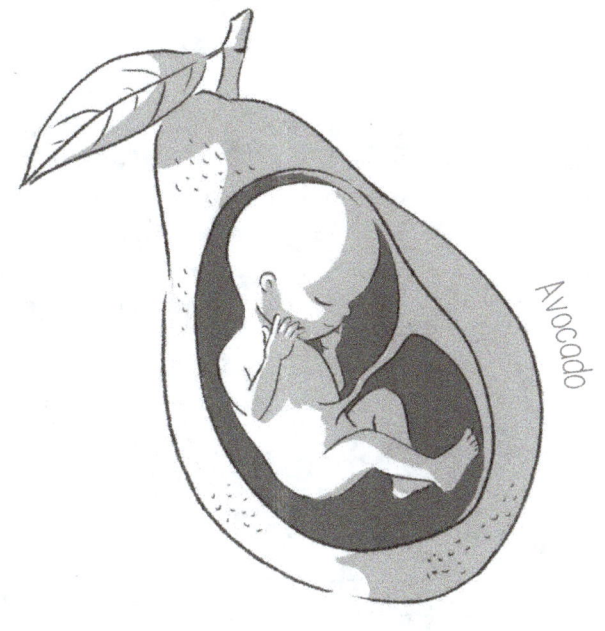

Avocado

WEEK

sixteen

day 106 connect

Your bundle of love is now responding to touch, showing that their brain is making connections with their muscles. At such an early age in development, the most important organ is performing a phenomenal feat. Just as the brain, or head, gives directions to the muscles for immediate response, pray today that your son or daughter will respond automatically to God's love in all circumstances.

Pray that your child will understand that obedience is better than sacrifice (1 Samuel 15:22).

Ask the Spirit to fill your little one's heart with God's love. As he or she comes to know God's love, your child will love Him in return. We love because He first loved us. Pray that love will result in obedience (John 14:15).

Pray that your child will not just be a hearer of God's Word but also a doer, responding in faith through works (James 1:22).

Momma,

Jesus sees all and knows everything. He loves His bride with a ravenous passion, and because He loves her, you can trust that He knows exactly how to sanctify and purify her. He speaks to her with overwhelming love, and she affectionately responds. What's her other option? Love is the only choice. Where do you need to see His love and pursuit again in your life? Jot down your thoughts as you pray.

day 107 humble

Your baby is fewer than five inches long from head to bottom and weighs about three ounces. Even at such a minute size, love for your baby has already filled your heart. When you think about how small your baby is, and contrast that to your love for him or her, it would be like comparing a drop of water in an ocean. This is your baby, your child. They haven't done anything yet or won any awards, but you still love them beyond measure. As you pray, think about the Lord's immense love for you and your child. Consider how weak and helpless you are without Him, and yet He loves you with all He is.

Thank the Lord that He regards your child in your humble, low estate (Psalm 136:23).

Praise God that He uses the weak and foolish things of the world to confound the wise (1 Corinthians 1:27).

Thank Him that His grace is sufficient for whatever your child needs. His power will be perfected in your child's weakness (2 Corinthians 12:9).

Momma,

One scheme of the enemy is to lie to you until you have a pity party. Once you open your heart and mind to thoughts about yourself that are not God's thoughts, you become a sitting duck for the unceasing harassment of the father of lies. He loves to torment you and make you feel small, insignificant, and unloved. The only thing that shuts his mouth is your belief. You can quote scripture to him, but that's not enough. Your faith, however, is a weapon. The Father wants you to be with Him so much that you come to believe Him because you know Him.

day 108 designed

How amazing is God's design that all our body parts fit together just perfectly, not too big, nor too small. Your baby's head will be proportionate to the rest of their body by the day of their birth. Today, as you're praying about your child's life, meditate on Romans 8:28: "We know that for those who love God all things work together for good, for those who are called according to his purpose." He will beautifully work everything for good for your son or daughter; you can rest in His promise that no trial or test will be wasted.

Thank God for the freedom found in Romans 8:28-29. Your child can have confidence that they are being shaped into the likeness of Jesus in everything.

Thank the Lord that He orders all things and holds all things together in the life of your child (Colossians 1:17).

Pray that your child will walk by faith, not by sight (2 Corinthians 5:7), not looking to the natural realm for answers and security but trusting God, who is able.

Momma,

How would you look at your circumstances if you knew they were perfectly designed by God to make you look like His Son? That's the heart of the Father: oneness and intimacy with Jesus, so that you become who you are beholding. Jesus gave up His own life not just to be a divine fixer of your problems but also so you could know Him in the midst of the problem. The difficulty loses its power to overwhelm you when you see Jesus in its midst.

day 109

glory

Your baby's tastebuds are developing quickly and even respond to bitter tastes in the amniotic fluid. Have you eaten something bitter lately? Your baby may have noticed. The Lord has given us the ability to respond to taste from the womb. Today, as you pray regarding this thought, consider when your child will face bitter circumstances. Ask God to empower them with mercy and goodness to overcome all evil.

Pray that your child will see Christ's grace is sufficient in all things (2 Corinthians 12:9).

Pray the Holy Spirit will flow out of your child like living water, blessing all those who come against your child because they know their battle is not with flesh and blood (Ephesians 6:12).

Ask the Lord to give your son or daughter His joy in fiery trials because there is a greater glory being prepared (1 Peter 4:12-19).

Momma,

Focus on your heart for a moment. Picture it in your mind. How do you see it? What images come to you? Now, whatever just came to your thoughts, ask the Lord to search them and know them. Did He show you some bitter offense you've been holding on to? He will never allow you to stay offended and get free too. He paid for that offense and wants to give you the heart of Jesus, who said, "Father, forgive them, they know not what they do." Do you trust Him to take that hurt and give you grace to not hold it against the offender? Think of what He gave to see you free, beloved—His very life.

day 110 hungry

Babies develop what's called a rooting reflex, where they turn in the direction of a slight touch on the cheek. This is especially noticeable after they are born and happens when they are hungry. Consider that gentle way a baby shows they are hungry, turning to you as the source of food. As you pray before feeding your baby, pray that he or she will hunger and thirst for righteousness in Christ (Matthew 5:6).

Pray your child will fix their eyes on Jesus, the author and finisher of their faith (Hebrews 12:2).

Ask that your child live by every word that comes from God, not looking only to food, or anything else in the natural, for satisfaction (Matthew 4:4).

Thank God that He is the supplier of every need of your child. He wants to meet every emotional, spiritual, and physical need and be the source of all provisions in your son or daughter's life.

Momma,

You understand hunger on a new level now. Some days you feel as if you could eat the proverbial horse, and some days the cravings send you headed straight to the freezer for ice cream. Hunger was created by God. Spiritual hunger can only come from Him because only He can satisfy it. How hungry for Him are you? He invites you, beloved, to feast on His faith, hope, and love. And if you're lacking hunger, thank Him for exposing that lack. Sit at His table again, expecting to be nourished by His grace.

day 111 praise

There are many changes taking place in your precious little one. Seemingly insignificant developments like toenails forming and more fluidity when they swallow are all miraculous. Every little change taking place in your womb is simply jaw-dropping. Seek the Lord as you think of these tiny miracles, asking Him to give your child a heart of praise. May your little one walk in worship and adoration of the Lord all their days.

Pray that your child will praise, bless, and thank the Lord for His goodness (Psalm 100:4-5).

Ask the Father to pour out His Spirit and blessing on your child (Isaiah 44:3).

Pray your child will worship in Spirit and truth (John 4:23-24).

Momma,

Everything becomes worship when it is done unto the Lord.

- Rocking a baby and meditating on the goodness of God: worship!
- Praying at the sink, drying towel in hand: worship!
- Blessing your family members in prayer as you fold the laundry: worship!

Renew your mind to see all these acts as times of love and adoration, not merely chores. They can be the sweetest times of thankfulness and pure worship as you abide in Him.

day 112 grounded

Your baby's foot is very distinguishable as a foot. It looks mostly like your mature foot. Without feet, the body cannot be stable. Feet give support so the rest of the body can have a foundation. In the same way, Jesus is our only sure foundation. In His life, our life is built. When trials come, pray that your child's security will be grounded in Jesus.

Pray that your child will be secure in God's love (Psalm 139).

Thank the Lord for the security He gives and how He surrounds your child (Psalm 122:7).

Ask that your child be filled with assurance of faith (1 John 5:13).

Momma,

What a deep, abiding comfort it is to know that Jesus is the same yesterday, today, and forever. Same. No changing, relenting, persuading, or flexibility. Jesus is our only security when seasons come and go. He alone is our constant. His love will not fade, be overdrawn, or exhausted. Be encouraged that you are completely safe and secure in Jesus.

Onion

WEEK

seventeen

day 113 mature

Your bump consists mainly of two things: your precious baby and amniotic fluid. The fluid is regenerated every few hours, although this process is little understood. Its purpose is to provide necessary nutrition and to cushion your little bundle of joy. They will soon mature beyond your womb. It's hard to imagine they will one day be fully grown and totally independent. Jesus designed us to grow and mature. He loves growing in His relationship with your child and knows exactly how to mature them from glory to glory.

Praise the Lord that He has perfectly gifted your child with spiritual gifts, which are given for helping grow the body of Christ (Ephesians 4:11-13).

Pray that your son or daughter will speak the truth in love and will grow up in every way in Christ (Ephesians 4:15).

Pray that your child will stand fully mature and fully assured of God's will (Colossians 4:12).

Momma,

Thank God for His grace during your maturing process. He is patient and longsuffering with you, and He waits on high to bless you (Isaiah 30:18). Become a lover of this process, not resisting His voice and leading. If the Holy Spirit shows you an area where He desires repentance, take heart; because He is going to bring freedom to that place. He wants you totally free from anything that would hinder you from receiving His love (Galatians 5:1).

day 114

grace

Your tiny baby measures about the span of your hand—around five inches from crown to rump. The number five is often a symbol of grace and abundance. As you reflect on the physical growth of your baby and their being covered in grace, let your prayers call down the favor of the Lord.

Thank God for His amazing grace, which covers every sin (Romans 5:2).

Bless the Lord, whose grace is sufficient for every circumstance in your child's life (2 Corinthians 12:9).

Thank God for the favor He gives your child to preach good news to the poor (Isaiah 61).

Momma,

What a miracle the Lord is knitting together in your womb. He surrounds you and your baby like a shield, guarding you with His Spirit. Surely goodness and mercy will follow you all the days of your life (Psalm 23). His grace is greater than any sin. If you sense condemnation well up in you, immediately turn to praise for the cross. Confess to Him your desire to become everything He paid for and then declare His love over yourself. Stay in the flow of thanksgiving and you will see the mouth of the enemy silenced. He cannot accuse the one who is humbled and seeking God's grace.

day 115   freedom

Babies prepare for life outside the womb by learning how to breathe in amniotic fluid; they develop the inhale-and-exhale mechanism. Breathing is essential for life. Consider the amazing design of God. He gave us not one but two outlets for breath—the nose and the mouth. When one is obstructed or blocked, the other one is critical for survival. As you pray for your baby today, ask the Lord to give him or her freedom to walk fully in the Holy Spirit, unencumbered by religious obstructions and mindsets.

As you lay your hands on your belly, pray your child will experience an anointing of the Holy Spirit. Where the Spirit of the Lord is, there is freedom (2 Corinthians 3:17).

Thank Jesus, who sets your child free from the law and curse of sin (Romans 8:2).

Pray that your child will walk in freedom, not using their freedom for the flesh but as an opportunity to serve in love (Galatians 5:13).

Momma,

When you think about the reality of freedom in Christ, what does that mean to you? Galatians 5:1 says He has set you free for freedom, but what does that actually mean? True freedom means that you are no longer held down by anything, such as anxiety, anger, or unforgiveness. Not one unrighteous thing has the right to rule in your heart any longer. The cross of Christ gives you freedom to love, and all things flow from His love in you. Your heart isn't tied to you any longer but rather to Jesus, who lives His life in you and through you.

day 116 wonderful

According to research, your baby may already be showing signs of their little (or big) personality at this time. Their personality is unique and God-given. The way they respond, perceive, and interact can be an exciting part of discovering the gift God gave you. Over seasons and time, you will see their personality develop and settle on their preferences, and you may even see your own personality emerge in them. You will have a deeper awe of how wonderfully He made you.

Praise the Lord that He knows and cherishes your child and that He created them wonderfully (Psalm 139).

Ask for Jesus to be reflected in the personality of your son or daughter and that they will always express His gentleness and kindness to those around them (Romans 8:29).

Ask the Holy Spirit to bear out His fruit in your child: love, joy, peace, patience, kindness, goodness, faithfulness, gentleness, and self-control (Galatians 5:22–23).

Momma,

Because you are in Christ, you have His mind and His thoughts. You are no longer bound or held to a certain type of personality, except that of the Holy Spirit, who is always loving and gentle. You bear His image, beloved, and your child will see their heavenly Father through you. God loves reproducing His image on the earth through His children. The whole earth is full of His glory (Isaiah 6:3).

day 117　　secure

Babies can now grasp objects. While tucked away in your tummy, there's no need for them to grasp anything, but one day their little hands will clench objects. Their ability to grab a pencil, a toy, and especially your hand provides help and security in their lives. Today, spend time praising the Lord who holds your baby securely in His strong hands.

Praise the Lord, who takes your child by the hand and calls them into righteousness (Isaiah 42:6).

Meditate on God's great keeping power because your son or daughter is held safely in His care (John 10:28).

Thank Jesus for His precious hands that bear the scars of the sins of your child (Psalm 22:16). He sets your son or daughter completely free by His death on the cross and resurrection from the grave.

Momma,

You may be familiar with the tune "He's Got the Whole World in His Hands," and while the title is true, it hits your heart deeply to realize it's you He's got in His loving hands. Those hands lift your weary head, wrap a robe of righteousness around you, and push the enemy away from you. How does He empower your hands on the earth? He uses them as instruments of love and service to everyone you see. Thank Him for blessing your hands, and ask Him to give you even greater grace to use them for prayer, healing, worship, and blessing.

day 118   held

Your baby's little arms are developing rapidly in form and function. His or her arm is a member of a body that embraces, lifts, and manifests strength. Your child's arms will be the very carriers of those first precious hugs. What a gift to be embraced. As you're praying over your child's arms today, praise the Lord that He stretches out His arm to you and your child in love and salvation. Take heart in knowing His able arms will carry your child throughout their life.

Pray your child will find their rest in the Lord's arms (Isaiah 40:11).

Ask the Lord to allow your son or daughter to become a mature believer who would bear up the arms of another and offer strength to a weary soul (Exodus 17:8-16).

Pray your child will know the Lord's arm is never too short to save them or anyone else (Isaiah 59:1).

Momma,

Today, lift your arms to the Father in worship and surrender. He will inhabit your praise and renew you with strength to love Him even more. Worship is such an important weapon for staying in a place of faith and peace. Keeping your heart and mind fixed on Him will enable you to see that God truly works all things together for your good. Worship is unique to you. Do you want to dance or sing as the Spirit moves your heart? He loves the way you love Him.

day 119   mind

The nerves and specialized parts of the brain continue to develop at this stage. It is hard to fathom that the brain's ability to accomplish different tasks at once forms at such an early age in your womb. Marvel at God's creative design today. He is, at this very moment, forming the same mind that will one day soon allow your child to process a boo-boo or experience butterflies in their tummy. As you spend time pondering the mystery of the human brain, thank God that He will be glorified through the mind and thoughts of your son or daughter.

Praise the Lord, who will keep your child in perfect peace as they set their mind on Him (Isaiah 26:3).

Ask that He would set your child's mind on the Spirit, not the flesh (Romans 8:5-8).

Thank the Lord that He has given your son or daughter the mind of Christ (Philippians 2:5).

Momma,

Love the Lord with all your heart, soul, strength, and mind (Luke 10:27). Draw close to Him today and yield your thoughts to Him. He will transform you by renewing your mind (Romans 12:2). He wants you to think like Him. Just like your baby will learn how to speak and walk, so, too, did you have to learn the new language of heaven when you were born again. You began to walk like Jesus and manifest His very mind in every circumstance, beloved.

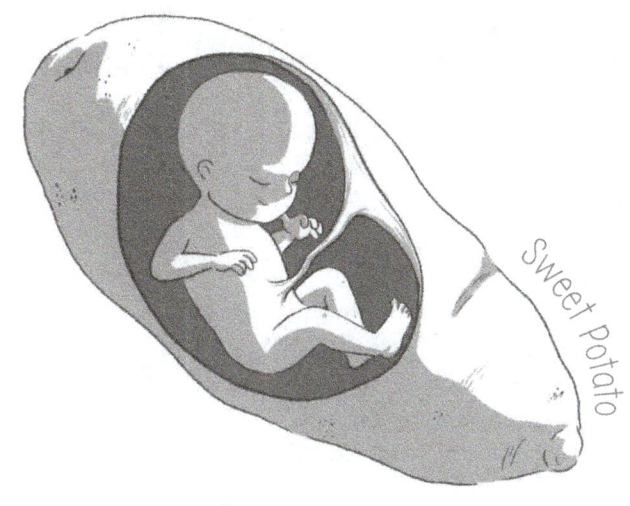

Sweet potato

WEEK

eighteen

day 120

alive

Your baby's many senses are in place, though still very immature. It is amazing to believe that even at fifteen weeks, your baby's abilities to hear, taste, touch, and smell have already manifested. These senses will continue to develop and literally cause your children to come alive as they experience the world around them. As you set your prayers on your baby's senses, pray that he or she comes alive in Christ, living at the impulse of His leading.

Thank God for His love for your child and for creating them perfectly in His image (Genesis 1:26).

Pray that they use their senses to glorify the Father, making their bodies instruments of righteousness (Romans 6:13).

Meditate on Ephesians 2:1-6, letting a prayer well up in your heart for your child: "You ... were by nature children of wrath, like the rest of mankind. But God, being rich in mercy, because of the great love with which he loved us, even when we were dead in our trespasses, made us alive together with Christ—by grace you have been saved (vv. 3-5)."

Momma,

When you were born again, you were made a brand-new creation, which means you died to yourself and Christ began to live in you and through you (Galatians 2:20). But what does death to yourself mean? It's total reliance on Jesus without any thought for yourself. Your former ways of living, thinking, and responding are gone. You are fully alive in Him, which means you're now aware of His presence, His life, His love. You don't just experience Him at church or occasionally while reading a devotion, but you can see, touch, and taste the goodness of Him in all things. Christ-life is even better than you knew.

day 121 covered

Your baby's bones are developing. These bones will also have marrow, which will create new blood in their little body. This process will change as they become an adult, when only certain bones will form new blood cells. Blood is the life-giving component of your body; it is literally the "tie" that binds all the organs together to function properly. As you're praying today, consider the precious blood of Jesus which was shed to cover and forgive every single sin on earth.

Praise Jesus for His life-giving blood that secures your child's salvation (Hebrews 9:12).

Thank the Father who freely offers His forgiveness for sin because of the blood of His Son (Hebrews 9:22).

Give thanks that you can intercede and approach God's throne boldly because of the sufficiency of Jesus's blood (Hebrews 10:19).

Momma,

Fix your mind on the powerful truths found in the hymn "Nothing but the Blood of Jesus."

What can wash away my sin?
Nothing but the blood of Jesus.
What can make me whole again?
Nothing but the blood of Jesus.
O precious is the flow
that makes me white as snow;
no other fount I know;
nothing but the blood of Jesus.

—Robert Lowry, United Methodist Hymnal, 1989

day 122 reveal

Your baby's gender can be determined at this early stage of development by a trained ultrasound technician. You might have been anticipating this surprise with great joy. Waiting to see if you're having a boy or girl stirs up expectancy and hope. Your son or daughter will be born for such a time as this, and God has amazing promises for the children in this generation. He says He will pour out His Spirit in the last days just before Jesus's return to earth.

Praise Jesus today that He will be revealed one day in His glory (Matthew 25:31).

Bless the Lord, who causes your child to be born again, and by God's power guarded through faith for a salvation ready to be revealed in the last days (1 Peter 1:5).

Spend time thanking God for strengthening your heart as you wait for Him to fulfill things that concern you (Philippians 1:6).

Momma,

Have you been guessing the gender of your baby? Whether you discover pink or blue now, or decide to wait until birth, your baby is already adored. You can be confident that the Father has purposes specifically for him or her. There are qualities unique to each gender, and God delights in the special ways He is forming His child. What do you love most about being a woman, a child bearer, a female? Don't fall into the trap of complaining about who God made you to be. Cast down lies of the enemy with truth and be free to live as His beloved daughter.

day 123   created

You may have noticed increased movement from your baby in the evenings. God designed your baby's brain with circadian rhythms, which naturally tell his body when it's day or night. As you think about the creativity of God, and notice His hand of detail in all things, spend time praising Him as your creator. He has created every single human life, complete with a body, soul, and spirit. How awesome to think you are carrying in your womb another eternal heart.

Praise the Lord for His promise that all creation will see His power and attributes (Romans 1:20).

Rejoice that God cares so deeply for His creation, lovingly and graciously providing for all its needs (Matthew 6:25-34).

Pray that your son or daughter will have a revelation of God as the creator of humanity and all the universe (Genesis 1:1).

Momma,

"Everything burns for your glory," a beautiful lyric in a worship song, testifies that your Father made all things for His sheer joy—including you. He made it all. Look up. Do you see the sun, the clouds, trees, your hands, your very breath? From the smallest iris of your eyeball to the greatest star in the sky, your Daddy created it all. Praise Him today that you are where He expresses His greatest glory because His Son manifests in you.

day 124
free

Your baby's digestive system is now working, which includes the stomach, although no solid waste has developed quite yet. The digestive system is vital to eliminate excessive waste from the body. Praise Jesus, who makes all things clean and new. When Jesus removes sin, we become free to truly walk in righteousness and abundant life.

Pray that your child will grow and mature in the knowledge of their freedom in Christ (Galatians 5:1).

Ask the Spirit to give your child a true revelation of their righteousness in Christ that is not based on outward works (Romans 10:4).

Pray that your children will guard their heart and know that all their words and thoughts find their source there (Luke 6:45).

Momma,

Lay all things bare before Jesus, including the deepest thoughts and intent of your heart. He knows you, beloved. He really, really knows you, even better than you think you know you. Meditate on that for a moment. He sees you complete in His Son and is looking at you as your future self. All your potential and everything you are becoming is His joy to behold. When He looks at you, His eyes catch the reflection of Himself.

day 125   walk

Have you felt your little one kick yet? Tiny legs will soon manifest light jolts, or kicks, which will feel like flutters at first. Your son or daughter will walk on those legs one day and will eventually be able to run. As you pray for those legs today, consider the spiritual implications of walking or running in faith. Jesus compares your journey of faith to a walk, growing one step at a time. Pray for your child's walk in Christ, that he or she will stay in step with the Spirit.

Pray your child will walk in love as Jesus commanded (2 John 1:5).

Pray your child will run with endurance the race set out before them and look to Jesus, the author and perfector of their faith (Hebrews 12:1-2).

Ask that your child will walk in the Spirit (Galatians 5:16).

Momma,

You will experience the fun and anticipation of seeing your child take its first steps one day. You will call his or her name, with your hands held out, asking him or her to let go of the side of the couch and come to you. You know those initial steps will have some falls, but still you encourage your precious little one to keep trying. Can you just imagine your heavenly Father calling your name to come to His loving arms? Your stumbling does not deter Him from His goal: that you will be established one step at a time, secure and sure-footed in His strong love.

day 126

Your baby's ability to make small, fine motions has been growing. Those tiny fingers will be free to move independently, all orchestrated by specific nerves in the brain. How useful a tool are hands. God created them for a variety of purposes. Giving a simple pat on the back or a hug can minister strength and encouragement to a broken soul. As you pray for your baby's hands, ask that your little one will use them to bless, pray for, and heal others.

Pray your child's hands and heart will be pure, washed by the Word of God (Psalm 24:4).

Praise God for always holding your little one up with His righteous, victorious hand (Isaiah 41:10).

Rejoice that God's good hand is on your child (Nehemiah 2).

Momma,

Is there anything more reassuring than the gentle hands of a mother? Look at your hands. As you inspect the glory of God's design, do you spy the place He put His own signature of your individuality—your fingerprint? Can you hear your Father saying, "I don't want another like you. I personally marked you and set you apart to be mine alone"? Hallelujah. His great love is branded on your fingers.

mango

WEEK

nineteen

day 127   walk

Your baby's touch sensation is developing. Already in place is their premature walking reflex. Your little one's "walk" in Christ will be led by the Holy Spirit and will mimic natural walking. Walking happens progressively by taking simple steps forward. Eventually, those steps happen with very little effort, much like walking in the Spirit.

Pray that your child will live by the Spirit and keep in step with the Spirit (Galatians 5:25).

Pray that your child will walk according to Jesus's commandments, the most important of which is love (Ephesians 5:2).

Momma,

Maybe your "walk" with Christ has felt like a slow crawl. Those times were purposed by Him to build up faith. Take heart! He is as much present in those seasons as He is in the times of vibrant running. Crawling is a position of humility. He teaches us that in our weakness, His strength is perfected (2 Corinthians 12:9–10).

day 128 presence

Dear Momma,

Today's devotion looks a tad different from the norm. As your baby continues to grow inside you, take some time to sit in the Lord's presence. Just sit and listen for a while. Move as the Spirit leads and then worship and pray. Be prepared, trusting with a full heart that He desires to draw you into His sweet presence. He operates in love, so meditate on His amazing love for you. If you've left your first love, He's been waiting to bless you, receive you, and pour out His grace on you. He sits in heaven, longing to show you His deep compassion (Isaiah 30:18). The Lord is so moved over you, His most precious creation. You are His child and He is your Father. He says He calls you by name and declares you are cherished and valued.

Have you had a revelation of His love? If you do not know the assurance of His mercy and love, confess your heart to Him. Pray in the Spirit, and always pray in faith.

Pen your heart to Him in your journal, beloved, and write your deepest desires. His presence may overwhelm you and bring you to tears. He may give you a new song, reveal His Word in a fresh way, or give you a picture or image in your mind that speaks to you.

day 129

move

Get ready! Your little one is moving all the time, although you may not be able to feel it. Maybe soon you will experience those quick flutters, technically known as quickening. Your little one will one day be on the move, and those legs will kick a soccer ball, swim in a pool, and climb stairs. As you consider the places your child will go, pray that they will move or quicken to the Lord's leading with an obedient heart full of faith.

Ask God to draw your child by love and awaken their spirit (Jeremiah 31:3).

Pray that your son or daughter will live, move, and have their being in Christ (Acts 17:28).

Rejoice in the Lord that your child can never fail in Christ but will know that He causes all things to work together for their good (Romans 8:28).

Momma,

Remind yourself that you are God's child and that He also disciplines you like a good Father. His promise concerning His discipline is twofold: He says it is sorrowful, but He also promises that afterward, it yields the fruit of righteousness. Hallelujah. It is hard to imagine your little angel will ever need correcting, but that sin nature will eventually manifest. Ask the best Parent for His wisdom, and He will give you the grace to discipline in love.

day 130 life

Your baby's source of nourishment, the umbilical cord, is also growing. It is a literal lifeline, linking your child's body to yours. This cord provides oxygen and nutrition, making it a necessary part of your child's development. Consider the function and importance of the umbilical cord. Jesus calls Himself a lifeline: "I am the way, and the truth, and the life" (John 14:6). He is your child's living source of life spiritually, physically, and emotionally.

Praise Jesus, who declares He gives your child abundant life (John 10:10).

Pray for your son or daughter to be filled with the Holy Spirit, who gives life and peace (2 Corinthians 3:6).

Ask that your little one grows in spiritual maturity, keeping their tongue from evil and producing life and goodness (1 Peter 3:10).

Momma,

Your heavenly Father never sleeps nor slumbers. His life is always energized and alive with vigor. May you experience His full life in you, beloved. Fatigue can result from working in the flesh or in your own strength. But as you are led by Him, He gives you the power to be productive in the call He's placed on your life. He created your body to rest, so do not confuse physical tiredness with emotional weariness. Confess your heart to Him today, asking Him to renew your life in the Spirit. He delights in doing so.

day 131 guarded

Your little one's sweat glands are being fashioned. Although they will not be needed for a while, these glands are a grand protection for the body. Sweating usually has a negative connotation, but without sweat your body would overheat. What a neat cooling mechanism, guarding your little one from potential danger. As you pray today, consider how the Lord guards your child in big and small ways. His love is a protection that continually guards their heart.

The Father is able to guard all that He entrusts your child's heart with (2 Timothy 1:12).

Praise Him for commanding His angels concerning your little ones, and for guarding them (Psalm 91:11).

Pray that your child will walk in the righteousness of Jesus that guards their mind (Proverbs 13:6).

Momma,

Did you know that you are securely guarded because your life is hidden in Christ? The enemy is often credited with being powerful, but there's too much focus on him robbing the rightful peace of the believer. Jesus says, "I give them [believers] eternal life" (John 10:28). When you're focused on the beauty of the beautiful One, why would you want to behold anything else?

day 132   hear

Your baby's little ears have already found their permanent position on their head. Your son or daughter's ability to hear with their heart is only possible by abiding in the Spirit. There is a difference between listening and hearing, and you desire your child to not be merely a hearer of God's Word but also a doer. Pray today for his or her spiritual ears.

Praise the Father for the distinct and beautiful way your child will distinguish His voice (John 10:27).

Rejoice that God will call your child and they will respond in obedience (Revelation 3:20).

Pray your child will experience faith that comes from hearing God's Word and learn that relationship is the primary way God wants to communicate (Romans 10:17).

Momma,

Train yourself to pay attention to what you hear. If you have a thought that leads to condemnation, guilt, despair, or hopelessness, that is not from your Father. If you experience His grace that leads to joy, repentance, and hope, you can trust you're hearing from God. So often you can let one lie linger in your heart and mind until another lie comes along, compounding the first lie over and over until a stronghold is fortified. Once a stronghold is established, the enemy traffics that place unless truth is proclaimed. Praise God, He demolishes the enemy's stronghold with His wisdom and then true freedom can reign.

day 133 fullness

Your little one will double their weight over the next few weeks. You're in good company if you've already gained some weight. Your baby gaining weight is a good sign of healthy growth and progression. The Lord designed your body to function at a normal, healthy weight. As you pray about how your sweet bundle is growing so quickly, stop and consider the perfect design of the Father. Moving forward with continual growth is His will for your child. He already sees them as completely whole and will spend a lifetime perfecting your little one in His image.

Pray your child will grow in the grace and knowledge of Jesus as Lord (2 Peter 3:18).

Ask the Father to grow up your son or daughter in every way into Jesus, who is the Head (Ephesians 4:15).

Thank the Lord that the gospel will bear fruit and grow everywhere your child goes (Colossians 1:5-6).

Momma,

Your Father God desires to move you from a measured to an abundant life. What does that mean? It's a life so full of the Spirit of Jesus that there will be no ability to measure it in natural terms. To live in fullness is to live in the presence of God, to simply abide in Him, being aware of Him moment by moment. He is your life, and He longs for you to partake of His (2 Peter 1:3-4).

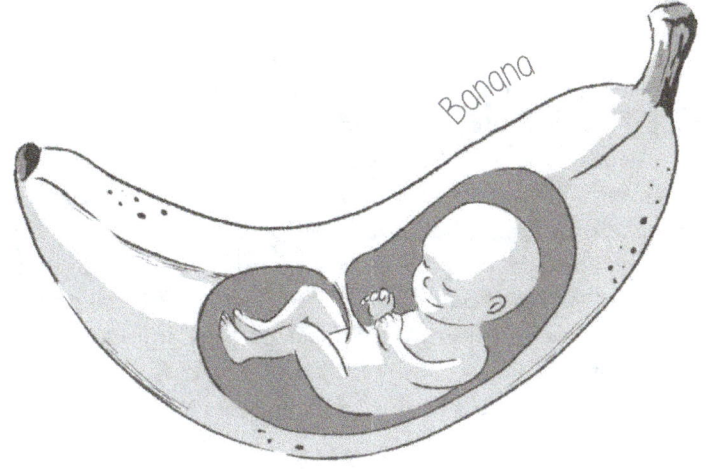

Banana

WEEK

twenty

day 134 ~ position

Your little one is nuzzled upright in your womb and probably has found his or her favorite spot under your ribs (at least, it feels that way). Your baby still has some growing to do before he or she emerges into the world, but you will know birth is near when a change in position takes place. Once he or she wiggles into a head-down position, your pregnancy days will be drawing close to your baby's birthday. Yay! As you pray for your child today, ask that God's love will be perfected in them as He perfectly positions them in the many seasons of life.

Praise the Lord, who declares the times and seasons and appoints all things in your child's life (Daniel 2:21).

Thank God for creating a season for everything and times for every matter under heaven. Rejoice that He is Alpha and Omega, knowing all the days of your little one and seeing his or her life from beginning to end (Ecclesiastes 3:1; Revelation 1:8).

Momma,

Have you read about the life of Joseph from the book of Genesis? God gave him prophetic dreams, and soon after, he found himself in a literal pit, left for dead at the hands of his own brothers. From then on, his life was a roller coaster of defeats, yet God would give him favor with each setback. Pretty soon, he was second in command in Egypt. One thing Joseph had consistently: faith in God's promise. And His Word is all you need for every circumstance. Jesus says, "Man shall not live by bread alone, but by every word that comes from the mouth of God" (Matthew 4:4). He sees your future, beloved, and longs to make you like Himself along the way.

day 135 — seed

If you've been blessed with a baby girl, your little one's genetic material is being downloaded into the eggs of her ovaries. Pray for your daughter, and if you're carrying a son, begin now to bless and pray for his wife. Consider the awesome way God is entrusting you with someone else's mother. Your baby will always be your baby, even if she becomes a momma herself someday. She will bear the seed for future generations, and the Father is allowing you to sow into her life through prayer.

Praise God that He has called your little one by name from before conception (Isaiah 49:1).

Praise the Father, who will put His Spirit on your son or daughter, causing them to prophesy (Joel 2:28).

Thank God for His awesome love because He declares, "I will be a father to you, and you shall be sons and daughters to me" (2 Corinthians 6:18).

Momma,

Seeds. Every fruit on the earth has a seed, and that's how they replicate themselves. The Father's perfect design is for you to carry His life and for the seed of His love to be replicated on the earth. Apples come from apple trees, planted by tiny apple seeds. You carry a seed in your womb, and soon, he or she will bear your image. He loves making you in His image, and He delights in bearing His love in and through you. He truly unites all things in Himself. How are you showing Him to others today?

day 136 strength

Your baby's bones are growing and calcifying or hardening. Their skeletal system will increasingly strengthen, and it will eventually provide the structure for the rest of their body. Their bones need to be strong so they can support their life-giving organs. Soft or brittle bones can be a sign of weakness, so as you're praying today, consider the strength of your child's spirit. If the strength of your little one is found in the Lord, they will not fail.

Pray the joy of the Lord will be your child's strength (Nehemiah 8:10).

Ask that your son or daughter will wait on the Lord and that they will renew their strength in Him (Isaiah 40:31).

Pray the Father will produce quietness and trust in your child's life, which causes strength to well up within them (Isaiah 30:15).

Momma,

What comes to mind when you think of strength? Do you picture yourself holding it all together, then falling apart behind closed doors? The grin-and-bear-it mindset is not true strength. True strength is joy and peace even in the midst of very pressing trials. Read the Gospels and see the strength of Jesus even when His circumstances were crushing. Be reminded of God's promise to Paul: "My grace is sufficient for you, for my power is made perfect in weakness" (2 Corinthians 12:9). He wants to be your strength today, beloved.

day 137 less

"Momma brain" is a real thing. Research shows that in the next trimester, many pregnant women experience a slight shrinkage in the brain due to hormones. You may find yourself needing to write down your grocery list and scrambling for missing car keys. But consider the parallel to the gospel: less of you and more of Jesus. If you become more forgetful, it will be a beautiful opportunity to grow in dependence on the Spirit. He delights in leading you and directing your life. He knows best how to lead you. Let Him gently bring you to the very end of your own life so you can find His.

Meditate on Proverbs 3:5–6: "Trust in the LORD with all your heart, and do not lean on your own understanding. In all your ways acknowledge him, and he will make straight your paths." Pray that your child will walk in the wisdom of God and not in their own natural understanding.

Pray that your son or daughter will have this mind: "He must increase, but I must decrease" (John 3:30).

Ask that your child will be led by the Lord, like a much-cared-for sheep. And even if danger is all around, that your child will know the goodness and security of the great Shepherd (Psalm 23).

Momma,

The Christ-life is summed up in Galatians 2:20: "It is no longer I who live, but Christ who lives in me. And the life I now live in the flesh I live by faith in the Son of God, who loved me and gave himself for me." Jesus is your constant supply of goodness, love, and peace. Your nature is His nature. Think of who He is, beloved. Beautiful, wonderful, patient, gracious, and full of every good attribute. What promise you have because He indwells you. What are your favorite things about Jesus?

day 138 rest

Babies are nestled securely in amniotic fluid, which creates the perfect place for them to begin a rest-wake pattern. The kind of rest our bodies need is important for healing, recovering, and growing. Consider the spiritual rest that is yours because of Jesus. You are forever free from the law and working for salvation, hallelujah. Pray your child will know the perfect rest of Christ.

Ask that your child will not only rest in God but will lead others to this refreshing rest as well (Hebrews 4:1-11).

Pray your child will find rest in Christ alone (Matthew 11:28).

Pray your son or daughter will take up the yoke of Jesus and learn from Him because He is humble and gentle. He promises to give rest to your child's soul (Matthew 11:29-30).

Momma,

Soon you will have a baby to cradle in your arms. Rest will give way to sleepless nights at first, but your spiritual rest can remain constant in Christ. In your weakness and sleeplessness, He can multiply grace. He will whisper to your heart, "Let Me be your peace. Let Me show you My strength as you cry to Me." He promises your thoughts will remain controlled by His life and peace as you set your mind on Him (Isaiah 26:3). There's never an exception to His Word.

day 139

peace

Your baby continues to develop their reflexes. Did you know that if your little one is startled, you may notice a distinct jolt or kick? God gives your body this instinct from the womb. As your child grows, pray that those instincts to defend or recoil will give way to peace and not alarm. The world knows the way of panic, anxiety, and depression, but God's portion is overwhelming peace that passes understanding. His glory is on display when you remain steadfast in His love while the world scrambles for answers. Thank God, who Himself is the Prince of Peace (Isaiah 9:6).

Ask the Spirit to guard the mind of your child, keep them fixed on things above, and to seat your child in heavenly places (Colossians 3:2; Ephesians 2:6).

Pray your son or daughter will respond to alarms with prayer and thanksgiving, and that God's promised peace will guard their heart and mind (Philippians 4:6-7).

Momma,

Peace has been described as the presence of Christ, not the absence of trouble. Jesus says, "I have said these things to you, that in me you may have peace" (John 16:33). A lack of peace means there is a lack of trust. This is not meant to condemn you, beloved, but rather to spur you to refocus. Change perspective. Look to Him instead of the circumstance. And once you lock eyes with Him, why would you want to be consumed with anything or anyone else? You will have peace as you stay focused on Christ.

day 140 crowned

How sweet to think your baby is already developing hair on the crown of his or her little head. Your little one may don a head full of hair at birth or be bald until toddlerhood. Even this detail of development creates such excitement and wonder for your baby's arrival. As you're praying for your little one today, consider earthly crowns. They often speak of royalty and heavenly rewards. The Lord crowns every one of His children's heads, making them royal sons and daughters of the King of Kings.

Rejoice, knowing there are crowns of righteousness already laid up for your child, which they will receive at the Lord's appearing (2 Timothy 4:8).

Pray that your child remain steadfast under trial, and when they have stood the test, they will be given a crown of life promised to those who love God (James 1:12).

Praise the great Shepherd—Jesus—who, when He returns, will grant an unfading crown of glory to those who shepherded His precious flock. Pray that God will raise your little one up to minister as an under-shepherd (1 Peter 5:4).

Momma,

Have you ever worn a tiara like the one given to a homecoming queen? Did you cherish that feeling, experiencing the glory of being a princess? That earthly trinket cannot compare to the heavenly rewards God has waiting for you. Imagine for a moment the bling and shine of God's crowns given to His sons and daughters. Those eternal crowns of glory, righteousness, and life will shine in great brilliance, reflecting the goodness of our God. What you do today matters. Is it eternal, beloved?

Pomegranate

WEEK

twenty-one

day 141

Your little one's brain is still being fashioned. It appears smooth compared to a wrinkled adult brain. The section of the brain that tells the hand to touch and to wriggle fingers has already developed. Receiving messages from the head is exactly the way we receive communication from God. He speaks through His Spirit in many ways: through His Word, other people, dreams, music, and anything else He chooses to use. Pray your child will respond in trust and surrender with every whisper of the Holy Spirit.

Just as Jesus was driven by the Spirit, pray your son or daughter will always be led by the Spirit (Mark 1:12).

Pray that your little one will be filled with the Holy Spirit, giving them loving discernment (Ephesians 5:18).

John 15:5 says, "I am the vine; you are the branches. Whoever abides in me and I in him, he it is that bears much fruit, for apart from me you can do nothing." Jesus longs for a relationship. Pray that your child will abide in Jesus, bearing much fruit.

Momma,

What you are doing at this moment for your child—interceding and praying in the Spirit—comes with the promise that fruit will be borne. Do not lose heart as you pray day after day. You're sowing eternal seeds that will reap rewards in the spirit. You are learning the very heart of the Father as you seek Him. When you pray, listen. Listen to His heart. Be still. That's abiding. When you turn upward toward Him and His kingdom, you will become more like Him, bearing His love in all you do.

day 142 harmony

Babies at this stage have fully formed eyes, although their eyelids are just beginning to separate. Their little retinas, corneas, and lenses are waiting for optic nerves to be completed. These parts will soon work in harmony, so your little one can see. All the parts of your body have been created to work in sync. The individual parts make the whole; they cannot function separately. As you pray over the eyes of your child, also think about how God wants them to build up the body of Christ, working together alongside their brothers and sisters.

Pray that your son or daughter will live in harmony with the family of God (Romans 12:18).

Thank God for giving your child endurance and encouragement to live with believers such that they glorify God (Romans 15:5-6).

Thank Jesus, who will bind everything in your child's life together in perfect harmony (Colossians 3:14).

Momma,

Music has healing qualities. What often soothes the soul is the harmony you're hearing of notes and rhythms blending together. Harmony is orderly, and a lack of it sounds obviously off to a listener. Harmony is defined as an agreement, accord, and harmonious relations, which perfectly describes what Jesus does—He restores our relationship with the Father, mingling our spirit with His and each other's, causing a beautiful sound to be heard on the earth. Redemption. What does it sound like to you?

day 143   hear

Your baby's ear, the external part, has reached a milestone: it has fully developed before birth. Your little one can hear sounds inside the womb and will be able to hear your voice clearly when you see them face-to-face. What wonderful things are you saying to your baby now? The Lord gives every human two sets of ears: physical ones and spiritual ones. Your son or daughter communicates with the Holy Spirit by listening with their spiritual ears. Pray that your little one will not just be a hearer of the Word but also a doer (James 1:22-25).

Pray that your child will know the voice of their Father as He speaks (John 10:1-5).

Jesus repeatedly talked to people who had "ears to hear" (Mark 4:23; Revelation 2:29). It may seem obvious that anyone with ears can hear, but He was speaking to those who have spiritually trained ears. Pray that your little one will tune in to the Spirit, obeying His leading.

Momma,

Faith comes by hearing and hearing by the Word of Christ (Romans 10:17). Your faith is produced as you listen in relationship with Him. God doesn't want you to merely read His Word. Jesus is the Word made flesh. As you read, your spirit is literally reading Him (John 1:1). You will see Him more and more as the Word shifts from a book to a person. He is both. Today, confess your desire to know His heart as you study His Word. Let the Spirit guide you into all truth (John 14:26).

day 144 surrounded

Your little one is surrounded in a fluid-filled sac called the amniotic shell. It helps maintain a regular temperature and also helps with your baby's development of muscle strength. The surrounding bubble provides a warm atmosphere where your baby can grow at just the perfect pace. As you're praying for your baby's growth, consider how the Holy Spirit surrounds your child like the sac. He loves to be involved in every detail of your son or daughter's life, strengthening, teaching, comforting, and enlightening along the way.

Praise the Father, who promises to give the Holy Spirit in abundance to those who ask (Luke 11:13).

Ask the Father to grant your child a life that is led by the Spirit (Galatians 5:16-18).

Rejoice that God desires to fill your son or daughter with all the fruit of His Spirit: love, joy, peace, patience, kindness, goodness, faithfulness, gentleness, and self-control (Galatians 5:22-23).

Momma,

You—like your baby—are surrounded by the Holy Spirit. He wants to cultivate such intimacy with you that you are assured of His presence in all things. He wants to fill you with Himself, so the fruit of who He is comes spilling out. Listen and give more attention to those small promptings. He is speaking to you. The thought of that person who crossed your mind randomly as you were driving home from the store is not random. Ask the Holy Spirit about them. Pray blessings on them. You may not understand why in your own reasoning, but He is working on their behalf as you pray. You are learning to hear His gentle whispers.

day 145 heart

Your baby's heartbeat has developed so strongly that you can hear it through a stethoscope on your belly. Those little beats signify that blood is being pumped and life is being sustained. Your little one's heart is literally the center of life, both spiritually and physically. Strong hearts are made in Christ alone. As your child grows in the Lord, pray for their heart to be strengthened, so they can thrive in all circumstances.

Praise Jesus, who strengthens your child's heart in grace (2 Timothy 2:1; Hebrews 13:9).

Thank the Lord, who stands with your child and strengthens them, even when they are forsaken by all others (2 Timothy 4:16-17).

Pray that your child will love the Lord with all their heart (Mark 12:30).

Momma,

The joy of the Lord is your strength (Nehemiah 8:10). Let the fullness of Jesus's joy empower your heart. He is confident of His goodness and work in your life, sanctifying you in all things. But do you wish for the circumstance to be over already? He wants to give you joy in the midst of it. There's no promise of joy after the trial is finished. It's in the middle of the test when you see strength rise and your joy being perfected. He is overcoming in you. Let Him have His way.

day 146   breath

You may have noticed a light, rhythmic sensation and wondered if that could be your baby's hiccups. Most likely by now, you can easily detect the phenomenon, which is actually preparing your baby for breathing outside your womb. Your tiny hiccups are your body's way of getting oxygen to the brain. You know that breathing is essential for life, so every inhale and exhale is significant. Consider the importance of using your breath to praise the Lord! Today, pray your child will breathe worship and affection for God.

Praise the Lord, who will cause **all** living things to worship Him because He is worthy (Psalm 66:4).

Ask the Father to give your son or daughter an eternal perspective, understanding their life is like a fleeting breath (Psalm 144:4).

Pray your little one will live by God's Word, breathed out by God Himself (2 Timothy 3:16).

Momma,

What's your natural default to stress? You have probably told yourself "just breathe" or "take a deep breath." Have you ever thought about why? Inhaling air slowly produces calm and control in the midst of hysteria. But that's not the answer Jesus gives for lasting peace. He promises to **be** your peace as you trust Him in the trials. In fact, He wants His peace to be so evident in you that others sense His calm in chaos. How are you expressing His peace today? Confess your anxiety as sin and thank Him for His grace to engulf you when you feel overwhelmed.

day 147 remember

Your little one's brain is still forming, even as you read this. The specialized part of their brain responsible for memory has already been working. Imagine all the memories you are going to make with your child. You will recall the early days of the birth, then toddlerhood, schooldays, and teen years. Your memories are a gift from God that reminds you of His grace and goodness over your life. It is important to God that you remember all the ways He has blessed you.

Praise God that when He saves, He promises to remember your child's sin no more (Jeremiah 31:34).

Thank the Lord, who is gracious and merciful, as He remembers your son or daughter's weaknesses (Psalm 103:14).

Ask God to search your heart. If a painful memory or relationship comes to your mind, pray for the Holy Spirit to grant you overwhelming forgiveness. The Father wants to heal that memory, so you can walk in freedom.

Momma,

In the Old Testament, stones of remembrance were set up, marking a time of God's faithfulness and deliverance. His children wanted to remember God every time they saw that stone structure. Beloved, you are filled with the Spirit of Christ. You no longer need a stone to recall God's goodness. His glory has filled you. The perfect sacrifice of Jesus is remembered throughout the earth when we tell His story of salvation (Luke 22:19). What is one of your favorite memories of His goodness?

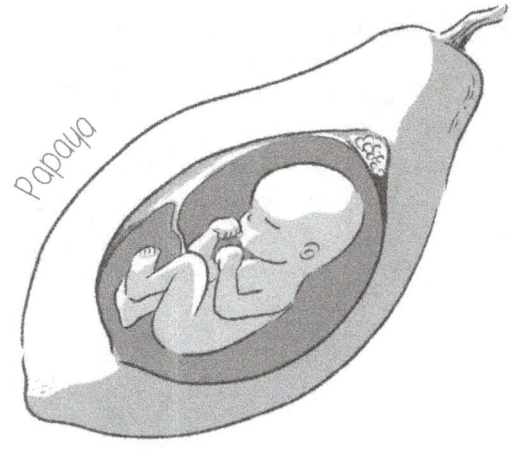

Papaya

WEEK

twenty-two

day 148   move

Your baby's little backbone is beginning to lengthen and form more stability for his or her body. The backbone or spine is the main support for the rest of the body. It serves as the connecting structure for the tissues, parts, and bones that are necessary for movement. Have you already dreamed of the ways your child will use their body? Will they be an athlete, kicking a ball around a soccer field, or a musician who sways to the notes played on a piano? Mobility is a gift from God. Pray today that your child will move according to the Spirit's leading in their life.

Praise the Lord, in whom your child will live, love, and have their being (Acts 17:28).

Pray that your child will have faith even as small as a mustard seed to speak to mountains and see them move (Matthew 17:20).

Ask that your child will follow the leading of the Holy Spirit with willingness and cheerfulness (John 3:8).

Momma,

Moving or living in the Spirit is the only place of true freedom. Living according to your own agenda keeps you in control, but God's way is better, and He desires to patiently increase your faith as you trust Him. Jesus offers vine life: your life rooted in His (John 15:5). The result is bearing supernatural power for love, joy, and grace, even in the midst of the mundane or a fiery trial. Surrender is sweet when we trust our Father is in control of every detail of our lives.

day 149

What a precious milestone! Your tiny baby's cochlea, the organ responsible for hearing, is complete and able to perform. Your little one is hearing your belly's gurgles and even your voice. Their heartbeat can even speed up when they hear your voice. Your voice is the clearest sound your baby hears because of bone conduction, and they can hear your heartbeat. Hearing and recognizing the tones and sounds of your voice is such a personal bond between a mother and her child.

Pray that your child will come to intimately know the voice of Jesus and follow Him (John 10:27).

Thank the Spirit, who speaks and calls your child to Himself by His voice (1 Samuel 3:4-10).

Ask that your child will always turn to hear His voice (Revelation 1:12).

Momma,

Your voice is unlike any other, especially to your child. Yours is unique, and its inflection will change often as a mom. They will learn your "momma" tone when being corrected, as well as your squeals of delight in proud moments. As you walk with God and read His Word, you, too, learn to not only know what He says but also how He speaks to your heart.

day 150 dream

Your hormones have shifted in pregnancy, which has caused an increase in your levels of progesterone. Because of this, you may have noticed you dream more when you sleep. Dreams are another tool God can use to speak to you. Not all dreams are from Him, but consider that He may want to communicate to you in this unique way. He often used dreams in the Bible to convey a warning or share His will. They can be symbolic or filled with mystery, much like a riddle. God loves for you to pursue Him, so ask if there's something He wants to speak to you through your dreams.

Praise God that He speaks to you even while you sleep (Job 33:14-15).

Thank Him for pouring out His Spirit in these last days. He promises to pour it out on all flesh, causing sons and daughters to prophesy, old men to dream dreams, and young men to have visions (Acts 2:17; Joel 2:28).

Momma,

What an exciting time to be alive. The Lord will pour out His Spirit in the last days. If you feel led, write down the things He is teaching you. You may consider keeping a dream journal as well. God wants to show you hidden things as you call to Him (Jeremiah 33:3). If someone gives you a prophetic word, test it against Scripture. What is He speaking to you in His Word? Do you sense a theme for this season of life?

day 151 humility

Your baby's brain is continuing to progress and grow. Certain chemicals are blocked and then released as the brain grows. As you're praying for your baby's brain today, consider that God's kingdom works on a paradigm. His way is not through great intellect or wisdom, but He works through childlike faith. He says that receiving Him only comes through simple belief. Pray that as your son or daughter matures in the Lord, their faith will become purified in humility.

Pray for humility in your child that manifests in their dependence on the Lord for salvation. Jesus says, "Unless you turn and become like children, you will never enter the kingdom of heaven" (Matthew 18:3-4).

Thank the Lord for the many ways He will speak to you through parenthood. You will experience a revelation of His love as you see the great love you have for your child. Rejoice in His love for you and your little one (John 3:16).

Momma,

Children are a blessing. They carry innocence and simple yet profound ways of thinking. Their cute responses, their ability to forgive quickly, and their witty perceptions about nature all bring glory to the Father. Children can sometimes send you running to your prayer closet because of their rebellious attitude. How do you maintain a peaceful home? In a word, grace. God will empower you with the same grace He parents you with. You are His beloved child. He loves being a Father to you. Do you regularly experience His delight over you?

day 152 strength

Your baby's grip is beginning to have noticeable strength. Although there's no need to grab a hold of anything in your womb, this ability will become important as they grow. Your child can soon carry objects, feed themselves, and grab your hand while crossing the road. God is so creative in His design to let your baby's hands and fingers grip. As you're praying today over your little one, ask that they know and hold fast to God always. He promises to never let go of His children.

Pray your child will hold fast to their confession of faith in Jesus (Hebrews 10:23).

Ask God to empower your son or daughter with genuine love so they abhor what is evil and hold fast to what is good (Romans 12:9).

Pray your child will take hold of the eternal life to which they are called (1 Timothy 6:12).

Momma,

When you hold your baby, remember your heavenly Father is holding you (Psalm 119:117). He holds you securely in His hands. He promises that no one can snatch you from His strong hands (John 10:28). Let your mind and heart dwell on that amazing reality. He loves you with a fierce and jealous love. Because God is for you, who can be against you? (Romans 8:31).

day 153 respond

Significant growth is happening in your baby's sensory development. When their little palm is touched, their fingers reflex. This reaction to a stimulus is a God-given gift. Touch will be one of the first ways you bond with your newborn. Skin-to-skin contact often creates a lasting bond from the start. Imagine the moment when your child's spiritual heart is touched by the love of the Father. Pray that he or she will respond with joy in surrender.

Thank God for His love for your child. Pray that as He draws your son or daughter, they will respond in love-driven obedience (John 14:21).

Ask that your child will recognize the voice of Jesus and the Holy Spirit at a young age (John 10:1-5).

Thank God that He chose your little one and that he or she is appointed to go bear fruit in His name (John 15:16).

Momma,

What choice do you have when you have a revelation of Jesus? His love is so irresistible that you cannot deny Him. Your only option is beautiful surrender. His perfect love overwhelms your heart, dissolving fear and doubt. Once you lock eyes with Him, your vision changes. You see the way He sees. You will never be the same, beloved. If you sense the weight of a circumstance or relationship is overshadowing your focus, ask Him to help you receive His love in a deeper way. He loves to love you.

day 154 *grace*

Your little one is starting to discriminate between flavors, swallowing more or less amniotic fluid each day based on its taste. The saying that you can catch more flies with honey than vinegar is true. When we use gracious, pleasant words, we manifest Jesus's attractive love to others and they want more. Your son or daughter will listen to your words and draw close to you depending on their "flavor." Your baby's first little words are the cutest, and you will hang on to every early babble. As they grow, those words will mature into sentences that express thoughts. Pray that your child will speak kind, honest, and loving words.

Pray that your child's speech will be filled with the grace of Christ (Colossians 4:6).

Ask that your child will speak kind words, bringing sweetness and healing to others (Proverbs 16:24).

Thank the Lord that He is merciful, slow to anger, and abounding in steadfast love (Psalm 145:8).

Momma,

You have been entrusted with this precious little one, and the opportunity for teaching, leading, and demonstrating will come through the most-used member of your body: your tongue. Ask the Holy Spirit to bless your speech with wisdom and your teaching with kindness (Proverbs 31:26).

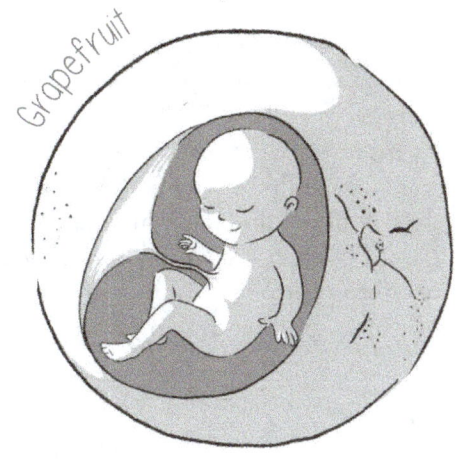

Grapefruit

WEEK

twenty-three

day 155 sonship

Your baby is becoming quite the wiggle worm these days. Their movements are continuing to reflect maturity and growth. Able to move freely now, they are exploring and stretching their body, becoming more familiar with how it moves. In the same way, moving in the Spirit is God's desire for them. Being led by the Holy Spirit, perceiving the direction He wants them to go, is a part of developing in the Lord. Hearing His voice can only be done in a relationship. Being a son or daughter of God and walking in intimacy with Him grows with time spent together.

Pray your child will walk in the Spirit and not satisfy the desires of the flesh (Galatians 5:16).

Ask that your son or daughter will be baptized in the Holy Spirit and bear the love, spiritual fruit, and varied gifts He supplies (Acts 19:6; Galatians 5:22-23).

Thank the Spirit, who will guide your child into all truth, bringing to their mind the words of Jesus (John 14:26).

Momma,

Jesus called the Holy Spirit "Helper." What a beautiful encouragement that you are never alone and that you have someone to constantly comfort you. This eternal Comforter and Helper dwells in you continually. He will give you wisdom and open your spiritual eyes to see His work in your heart. Where do you need to confess you actually need help? He already knows, beloved.

day 156 free

You are almost in your fifth month now, meaning your baby has put on more weight recently; they weigh about ten ounces and are the length of half a ruler from crown to rump. Are you imagining him or her, so tiny and fragile? Your doctor or practitioner will soon measure your baby to make sure they are growing at a healthy rate. You probably can confess you've also put on some pounds, making your baby bump more of a reality. Just like too much weight is unhealthy, spiritual weights or bonds can hinder your ability to run the race set before you. Pray that your child will not entangle themself in the burdens of life but will trust the Lord to carry them.

Pray the Lord will empower your child to lay aside every weight and sin, so they can run their race with endurance (Hebrews 12:1).

Praise God, He sets His sons and daughters free from bondage in order that they may obtain glory as His beloved children (Romans 8:21).

Praise Jesus, who sets your child free. Pray that your son or daughter will not submit to the yoke of slavery and will stand firm (Galatians 5:1).

Momma,

Isaiah 61 is your banner reality. The Lord has come to set you free from every yoke. The very places the enemy occupied are now where the light of Jesus shines. Hallelujah. There are no captives in His kingdom except those held by His perfect love. What a joy to rise above every weapon formed against you and use your weakness to display God's strength. Jesus defeated sin, death, hell, and every wicked thing. His blood has covered you completely: past, present, and future. This is where all your confidence rests—in Him in you.

day 157 see

Your baby's eyes notice light, and their eyes move slightly in response to bright lights outside your body, even though their eyelids are still closed. Their ability to see color will happen around the fourth month **after** birth. Until then, your child will see you in a sharp contrast of black-and-white images. Your son or daughter's spiritual vision will develop as they grow more Christlike, seeing the way He sees, through the lens of faith. Pray that your little one will not be led by their natural sight but by the always-hopeful perception of the Spirit.

Praise Jesus, who gives sight to blinded eyes, literally and spiritually (John 9).

Ask that your son or daughter be blessed with spiritual eyes that see Jesus and the truth of who He is. Pray that they will be voices of freedom to those who are spiritually blind (Isaiah 61).

Pray that your child will be born again, seeing the kingdom of God in all its fullness (John 3:3).

Pray that your child will fix their eyes on things above, not on things of the world (Colossians 3:2).

Momma,

John 9 is a prophetic picture of us. Although a man was born blind, Jesus gave him sight. Apart from Jesus, you cannot see. You are blind to the things of the Spirit—eternal things like mercy, truth, and hope. Touch your eyes (go ahead, no one is looking) and ask God to bless your spiritual eyes. Ask Him to open your eyes to see others the way He sees them. Ask Him to widen your vision for His Word, to see only through the lens of His truth. Pray that He will let you experience the glory of His perception from heaven, where you are spiritually seated. What do you see?

day 158 · voice

What a precious milestone your baby has reached: the cochlea, the organ responsible for hearing, is completely structurally formed. Think of all the sounds your little one hears right now. They hear each gurgle of your hungry belly and every conversation you have with a coworker. The bond being formed between you two is special, and your baby will recognize your voice at birth. The Father wants your child to recognize His holy voice as well. Pray that your little one will quickly perceive when God is speaking.

Pray that your child will intimately know the voice of Jesus and follow Him (John 10:27).

Thank the Spirit, who speaks and calls your child by name (Isaiah 43:1).

Ask that your child will know personally that "the voice of the LORD is powerful; the voice of the LORD is full of majesty" (Psalm 29:4).

Momma,

Your voice is unlike anyone else's. Your child will learn to recognize your joy or disappointment based on your tone. Your voice will change depending on each circumstance. Sometimes a whisper will do, while other times you will raise your voice in joyful delight. You may deepen it when correction is needed. He or she will sense your mood just based on your voice. A stern "Don't touch that" or a joyful "I love you" is what makes your relationship with your child special. You will learn the voice of Your Father, too, as you grow in intimacy with Him. You'll sense, even in correction, His gentle love and affection for you, daughter.

day 159

The end of the month will mark a milestone—your baby will have all his or her faculties to hear external sounds. Those teeny ears will soon be able to distinguish sounds like a dog barking or a joyful, boisterous laugh. They will find comfort in the way you sing over them at bedtime, while the vacuum hum may startle them. The ability to discern between good and evil will be both a safeguard and a joy to your child as they mature in Christ.

Thank God for His perfect wisdom and His promises to give it in abundance as you seek Him. Ask Him to grant your child wisdom as they develop friendships (James 1:5).

Praise the Lord who calls your child from birth to know Him. The call on their life is to become like Jesus, through a saving relationship with Him. Pray that they will discern between spiritual light and darkness through a knowledge of God's Word and the Spirit (Ephesians 5:6-10).

Momma,

You are called the light of the world, daughter. Your ability to discern between good and evil is the only hope for the world. As the church is increasingly mocked, discerning between the true wisdom of God and the foolish wisdom of the world is literally black and white. Hide His truth in your heart daily by receiving fresh "manna" from heaven. He will give you wisdom so that you're able to brilliantly shine in the midst of the darkness.

day 760 dependence

Imagine being in a warm bath continuously. Your little one is thriving in your womb because God designed your body to regulate your temperature so that your baby does not get too hot or cold. You may not think much about your body staying a perfect 98.6 degrees, unless you're sick. The master designer created your baby to depend on you while they grow. Just like you eat healthy food, drink lots of water, and rest—for a healthy body—God knows that you must depend on the Holy Spirit to stay healthy spiritually. Pray your son or daughter will cultivate a need and dependence on the Spirit's help in all circumstances.

Ask the Father to empower your child to be hot with Holy Spirit fire, full of His love and humility, and cool with refreshing grace and works that glorify Him (Revelation 3:15).

Pray your son or daughter will walk in full dependence on the Father as their source for everything, not growing lukewarm in self-sufficiency.

Momma,

What's the temperature of your heart? That question is not intended as condemnation but rather examination. Are you growing warmer in your love and adoration of Jesus day by day? His desire for you is to grow even more in love with Him and His Word, so your heart will continuously burn with flames of faith. Look to Him in prayer today, and lay your heart before Him. Confess to Him, "Here's my heart, Lord; it's Yours. Fill it with fresh anointing of the Spirit so that I don't grow cold." Amen.

day 161   abide

Where did you go for lunch today? Your favorite taco place? Maybe you're staying away from spicy foods, but your baby can possibly taste a hint of what you're eating these days. What you choose to eat has an effect on the taste of your child. They may grow up loving your favorite flavor of ice cream simply because they experienced it so young. Momma and baby are two complete individuals, but that umbilical cord is a link, literally tying you together. What a perfect illustration for abiding in the Father. Pray your child will abide in the Lord and He will abide in your child.

Thank the Lord for being the Vine who bears out fruit in your life (John 15:5).

Pray your child will abide in the love of the Father (John 15:9).

Praise God, who knows your child intimately and longs to dwell in their heart (John 14:17).

Momma,

Pregnancy is a beautiful picture of the Christ-life. You and your baby are inseparable right now. Your baby is literally dwelling inside you. In the same way, Jesus dwells in you—Him in you and you in Him. You can never be separated. Let the truth of Romans 8:38-39 reassure your heart today:

I am convinced that nothing can ever separate us from God's love. Neither death nor life, neither angels nor demons, neither our fears for today nor our worries about tomorrow—not even the powers of hell can separate us from God's love. No power in the sky above or in the earth below—indeed, nothing in all creation will ever be able to separate us from the love of God that is revealed in Christ Jesus our LORD.

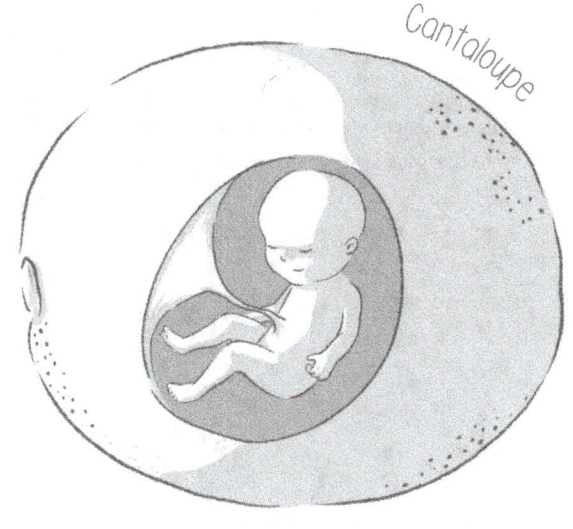

Cantaloupe

WEEK

twenty-four

day 162

praise

If you could peek inside your womb today, you would possibly see your baby crease his or her sweet lips to mimic a kissing expression. You are anticipating kissing those baby lips, but consider all the other ways your lips are important. They are the primary instrument used for praising God. You bring much joy to the Father when you worship Him with the fruit of your lips in prayer, worship, and thanksgiving. Pray your child will live a life of contagious praise, always bringing glory to God with their mouth.

Pray your son or daughter will shout for joy and pour forth God's praise (Psalm 20:5).

Pray your little one will offer up sacrifices of praise to God, the fruit of lips that acknowledge His awesome name (Hebrews 13:15).

Praise God that He will once again fill the mouth of your child with laughter and their lips with shouts of joy (Job 8:21).

Momma,

Your praises attract the heart of God. Imagine your child telling you all day how wonderful and loved you are; your heart would be filled with unimaginable joy. God says He inhabits your praises (Psalm 22:3). There are times for quiet reflection and meditation on His goodness, and then there are moments for shouting about His love. Jesus says that if you refuse to worship Him, rocks will begin to cry out. God isn't glorified by rocks but through His sons and daughters.

day 163 power

Your baby's circulatory system is fairly easy to spot right now. Because their skin is so thin, your little one appears red from the blood flowing through their capillaries. Your baby's body already needs blood for life. They carry nutrients and oxygen all around their tiny body from your placenta and umbilical cord, and they send back their deoxygenated blood and waste products the same way. As you pray today, consider the most powerful blood that has ever been shed, Jesus's blood on the cross. His blood covers every single sin and powerfully cleanses your heart and life.

Praise the Lord, who has justified your child by His own precious blood, making your son or daughter a completely new creation in Jesus (Romans 5:9; 2 Corinthians 5:17).

Thank God that by Jesus's blood, He made peace with your child (Colossians 1:20).

Rejoice in the Lord who loves your son or daughter and has freed them of the curse of sin (Revelation 1:5).

Momma,

Is there anything more powerful than the blood of Jesus, which washes you whiter than snow? (Psalm 51:7). It's His covenant-sealing blood that He gave to set you free. Just like your physical body cannot survive without blood, your spirit won't come alive until the blood of Christ saves you. Meditate on your complete freedom today (Galatians 5:1). He paid the highest and dearest price of His own life, beloved.

day 164 — anointed

Your baby's brain is continuing to mature and will soon have its familiar wrinkled, gray appearance. Those wrinkles are important for storing their millions of neurons being created daily, which transmit information to the rest of the body and tell your child when there's pain, pleasure, heat, and cold, and they send other important signals. As you pray for your little one today, think of how one day he or she will become part of the family of God. The Lord transmits His will to His body through His Spirit. Your son or daughter will be connected to Jesus, the Head of the body, making Spirit-filled connections with other believers possible.

Praise the Father, who did not leave your child alone but sent the Holy Spirit, the Helper, to teach him or her all things (John 14:26).

Pray for your child to do good to everyone, especially to those of the family of faith (Galatians 6:10).

Ask that God will allow your child to be sharpened like iron and to be a source of strength to others for mutual growth and upbuilding (Proverbs 27:17).

Momma,

You cannot forget your favorite schoolteacher. He or she was most likely fun or extraordinarily kind. The Holy Spirit is the teacher of all teachers; He instructs you in a personal way, patiently and lovingly showing you how to live in Him. Think of each season in your life as a mini graduation, being promoted from one degree of glory to another in His image (2 Corinthians 3:18). What is He currently teaching you?

day 165 — light

Your baby's eyes are the focus of your prayers today. The basic structures of their eyes have formed, including the retina, lens, and optic nerve. The retina, which is responsible for dilation, is the part of the eye where light is adjusted. God designed your eyes to work much like a camera lens; when it senses too much light, the retina closes. What a perfect provision. Consider that Jesus is the true light. He is the brightest light, dispelling all darkness. Pray that your child's spiritual eyes will discern Him as the way, the truth, and the life (John 14:6).

Praise Jesus, who calls every one of His children the light of the world (Matthew 5:14). Pray that your son or daughter's heart will be overcome by His light.

Thank Jesus that He clothes your little one in armor of light (Romans 13:12).

Thank God for giving you and your child His Word as a light for your path (Psalm 119:105).

Momma,

Bless God for the simplicity of the gospel; light came to cast out the darkness (John 1:1–5). Jesus is light, and He illuminates hearts, displacing the kingdom of darkness. The old hymn "Be Thou My Vision" declares "Be Thou my Vision, O Lord of my heart; / Naught be all else to me, save that Thou art. / Thou my best thought, by day or by night, / Waking or sleeping, Thy presence my light." If darkness is the absence of light, then where does He need to shine in your own heart and mind?

day 166 comfort

Your baby's eyelids are still closed, so, fortunately, he or she is not continually looking around at the same scenery in your womb. The glands responsible for tears have formed but do not yet work, and they will not produce tears until your baby is two or three months old. Although your heart breaks to hear your baby cry, those cries are important signals for "I'm hungry, Momma" or "My diaper needs changing." Don't worry; those kinds of cries will not appear for several months.

Thank the Lord for promising those who sow in tears that they will reap with shouts of joy (Psalm 126:5).

Be encouraged, beloved, that God collects all your child's tears in a bottle, recording each one in His book (Psalm 56:8).

Rejoice in the Lord, who promises that He will wipe away every tear from your face (Isaiah 25:8).

Momma,

Do you just need a good cry? Shedding some tears is cleansing. Not all cry sessions are because you're sad. Some tears well up from a thankful heart. Some tears are an immediate response to God's goodness. You can't help but let them pour from your eyes. Beloved, even Jesus wept (John 11;35). What's on your mind today? Be comforted to know that your Father sees every tear and hears your heart's cry even before you speak a word.

day 167 — life

Up until now, you may not have ever considered the miracle of your placenta. It is the thick muscle that surrounds your baby, providing nutrition, delivering oxygen, and managing waste. It also produces important hormones for your pregnancy. God is so creative in His provisions. The placenta is necessary for your baby's life. As you're praying today, meditate on Jesus being the source of spiritual life. In Him, your spirit is made new, and He lovingly provides everything you need. He promises not just life but also abundant life to those who trust Him.

Thank God for being such a loving Father by giving His only Son so your child could have true life (1 John 5:12)

Pray that your son or daughter will experience Jesus's abundant life daily (John 10:10).

Ask that your child will walk by the Spirit, which produces life and peace (2 Corinthians 3:6).

Praise God for granting a crown of life to your child as they remain steadfast under trial (James 1:12).

Momma,

What a simple freedom it is to trust Christ for everything. If you need peace, it is found in the Prince of Peace (Isaiah 9:6). If you need love, He is love (1 John 4:7–8). If you are craving rest, He is the giver (Matthew 11:28). You may be striving to find peace, love, or rest in your circumstances, but, beloved, you were created for a relationship. A lack of these things means a breaking in faith with Jesus. He is jealous for you and longs for you to trust Him as you come to Him. Everything else is shifting sand—fading and temporary. In Him is true life, and it's His joy to give Himself to you.

day 168   hungry

On an ultrasound, your little one can be seen making sucking motions that have become more coordinated with their swallowing. Their little reflex is getting ready for feeding. The sucking reflex is simple but necessary. Your little one will eat almost immediately after birth and will continue being hungry every couple of hours. Within months, the feedings become more regular, and you will watch your baby grow right before your eyes. You will be amazed by how much your baby grows in their first year of life. Spiritually, God uses your physical growth to imitate what He longs to do in you spiritually. He is wholly committed to the spiritual progress of your child, never taking a moment off from His shaping of their heart.

Thank the Lord of wisdom who promises to give you Himself as you need Him. He's so kind; He gives you wisdom without shaming you (James 1:5).

Pray that your child will grow into spiritual maturity (1 Corinthians 14:20).

Ask the Holy Spirit to empower you to teach your child and mold their mind so you can present them mature in Christ (Colossians 1:28).

Momma,

As you focus today on growth in the Lord, imagine that your heart is a beautiful tree. The only way for that blooming tree to grow even more is to prune it. Jesus says that those who produce fruit will be pruned in order to bear even more. When you think of pruning, your heart may recoil. Pruning involves cutting away the dead branches or stems to increase growth. Some pruning even involves training a plant to grow in a certain pattern. Beloved, let the Vinedresser have His perfect way in your life (John 15). He desires you to become as beautiful as Him.

Cauliflower

WEEK

twenty-five

day 169

delight

Your baby now measures 10.5-11 inches from crown to rump and weighs about 14 ounces. Their ability to respond to noise is increasing. Loud music and noises can cause sudden movements in your little one, some of which you may have already experienced. When those little kicks happen, their heart rate naturally increases. Imagine, now, the same response when God calls your child to salvation. The Holy Spirit will speak to your son or daughter, causing their spiritual heart to burst into life and ever increase in love for God.

Pray your child will surrender their heart to God and always delight in His ways (Proverbs 23:26).

Thank the Lord that your son or daughter will delight in Him and He will give them the desires of their heart (Psalm 37:4).

Praise God for His purifying work in the heart of your child, which empowers them to see Him (Matthew 5:8).

Momma,

Read the Song of Solomon and you will understand the thrill Jesus has when He looks at you, daughter. Can you imagine the Lord's heart beating a tad faster when He considers how wonderful His creation is? Get ready, because you will experience the same emotions when you finally behold that little one growing inside you. Your love will explode beyond expression, except often spoken in happy flowing tears. It's joy-full, and nothing on earth can compare with it. You are proud and happy and totally in love all at once. That delight is your heavenly Father's love for you.

day 170 distinguish

Your little one is already demonstrating complex skills, like the ability to distinguish new sounds from familiar sounds. Wow! Of all the sounds babies hear from the womb, your voice is the most distinguishable because it's the one they hear most often. After nine months, the sound of your voice has become so familiar that newer sounds, like those of siblings, will take some learning. Your voice, Momma, is the one your babies will listen to for comfort. You can soothe them like no one else. What a beautiful bond God has already created.

Praise Jesus for speaking to your child and conditioning them to know His voice (John 10:1-5).

Ask the Father to give your son or daughter spiritual ears to hear so they discern His still, small voice (1 Kings 19:11-13).

Pray your child speak only what they hear the Father saying (John 5:19; 12:49).

Momma,

Discerning the voice of Jesus can take practice. Here's one sure way to know you're hearing Him: His voice is full of love and grace. Pay attention to what you're hearing. If you're sensing guilt well up, that's not your Father. He speaks wisely and often directly to your heart through His Word. He is calling you to simply be still and know that He alone is God (Psalm 46:10). Shhh, quiet your heart. Clear your mind. Still your soul. Be content to say nothing and do nothing but sit in the peace of His presence. You will soon hear His gentle whisper of love.

day 171 confess

Your little one's teeth are developing. The outer covering of the tooth, the enamel, is starting to solidify. You probably won't see those pearly whites for months after he or she is born, but that gummy smile will light up the room. Those teeth will prove a milestone, coming in one by one, helping him or her to chew food. Soft teeth are a sign of weakness and decay, but the stronger the teeth, the healthier your little one is. Today, as you pray, ask for the opposite in your son or daughter's heart—that it be soft and pliable, not hard and full of unforgiveness.

Praise Jesus for His forgiveness and freedom from guilt as you confess your sin to Him (1 John 1:9).

Thank God that He will place people in the life of your child who will exhort them and that He will not allow their heart to be hardened by sin's deceitfulness (Hebrews 3:13).

Ask the Father to give your child a tender heart and brotherly love (1 Peter 3:8).

Momma,

Your heart is, in essence, your soul; it's the source of your emotions and will. Your emotions are a wonderful gift, but you're not to be directed by them. You were created to live from the Spirit upon salvation, not from your soul. Think of how wonderful feelings can be when you're happy but how destructive they can be when you're angry. Praise God that, in His perfect wisdom, He gives you another way to live—in Him. When you become His child, you grow in intimacy with Him, become like Him, and respond like Him. You don't become a robot with no feelings or will but rather a lover of Jesus. As you're changed into His image, your life will look like His, filled with love, joy, peace, patience, kindness, faithfulness, goodness, and self-control.

day 172 remember

You will be delighted to know that studies have shown babies may have the capacity to remember, even this early. They are able to distinguish what is familiar based on their sucking reflexes. Think of all the ways a memory can be triggered—through a smell, a taste, or simply the way you felt when that memory was made. God gives you memory as a gift. He wants you to recall His goodness and love over your life. Pray for your child to always remember God's faithfulness.

Thank the Father, who does not remember your child's sins because of the blood of Jesus (Hebrews 8:12).

Pray your little one will always remember and live in the power of Jesus's death and resurrection, which brings healing to the body, soul, and mind (Luke 22:19).

Pray that your son or daughter will become aware of God's presence in their youth (Ecclesiastes 12:1).

Momma,

Remembering moments in your life can cause emotions that span the spectrum from joyful to sad. One of the most freeing thoughts is that the blood of Jesus rights all wrongs. It can even cleanse memories, not necessarily undoing what was painful but cleansing the sting. Jesus can heal your perspective so you can see the circumstance the way He sees it. When you see everything through His shed blood, all wrongs become right. God's goodness overwhelms you with a new way of seeing and perceiving, so that He is glorified in all things.

day 173 — hidden

Today, Momma, remember that your little one is being hidden in your womb the same way you are hidden in Christ. Just as your baby is growing and developing day by day, so are you in Him. You are being changed from glory to glory (2 Corinthians 3:18).

Your prayers today will be centered around your heart. Meditate on your life in God. Jesus describes it in John 15:5: "Whoever abides in me and I in him, he it is that bears much fruit."

Be still and know that He is God (Psalm 46:10). Your heart needs Him more than your mind can comprehend. Don't rush time in His presence. Jesus was intentional about being with the Father. He knew that His life literally depended on it.

Beloved, begin to renew your mind to the truth: Christ in [your name], the hope of glory (Colossians 1:27).

Momma,

In the same way your baby is the fruit of intimacy, your life will bear fruit pleasing to God as you seek intimacy with Him. Allow His love to draw you deep into His heart. Put your phone away. Turn off social media. Get alone and get quiet. He promises to lure you into the wilderness (Hosea 4), where, in the most unexpected of all places, He will give you fruit. When you have Him alone, the things of earth will never satisfy. Relationships, possessions, and all the social media likes fall short. You will come to know Him as the only One able to give you the true desires of your heart.

day 174 — mature

Your baby's brain is already showing growth patterns. From the womb until they reach full adulthood, your child's brain will increase in complexity and be able to accomplish more intricate tasks. You were not designed to stay a child throughout life; God created you to grow into maturity and responsibility. Your little one won't be able to drive a car or read a novel for many years, but those are pleasures you can experience because you've grown into them. As you pray today, ask the Father to mature your son or daughter in Him and grow him or her in faith and trust.

Thank God that He will cause your child to be firm in faith (Isaiah 7:9).

Pray your son or daughter will in time leave the elementary doctrine of Jesus and move on to full maturity, lacking nothing (Hebrews 6:1).

Pray your child will be an infant "in evil, but in [their] thinking be mature" (1 Corinthians 14:20).

Momma,

Your sweet young child will have simple ways of thinking. As you hear their thoughts about creation, life, or their little world, God will often use them to speak profound truths to you. Children offer up the most powerful, innocent prayers to the Lord. Jesus tells you to come to Him with faith like a child (Matthew 18:3–4) because He knows you cannot reason your way to Him. He wants you to believe Him just at His word. You are going to learn so much just by watching your little one.

day 175   rest

Your baby is already developing a sleep pattern. Increased brain and eye activity are an effect of deep sleep. Growth requires rest, and your little one is growing by the hour. God rested on the seventh day of creation, not because He was tired but because He was finished with His masterpiece. God promises that He does not grow weak or tired, and He created us to walk in His spiritual rest. Just as your child's body requires physical rest, pray that he or she will live in the abundant spiritual rest of Jesus.

Praise Jesus for offering rest to the weary and heavy-laden. Pray your son or daughter will experience His rest and not look to the world for relief (Matthew 11:28).

Pray your child will walk in a continual rest and not strive in their flesh (Hebrews 4:9–10).

Thank God today for how His rest declares His love to the world. He is not a demanding God who exacts works and sacrifices from His children.

Momma,

Take a few moments and let the Holy Spirit speak to your heart. The first four letters in "restoration" spell R-E-S-T. It is essential you learn to live in peace, declaring the truth found in the hymn "It Is Well": "Whatever my lot, / Thou has taught me to say, / It is well with my soul."
The enemy wants you to be anxious, beloved. He wants you to be driven by fear in all your decisions and responses. Remember, he is a liar and a thief. But nuzzle up in the broad love of Christ and remain there. Why would you ever want to leave Him? In Him, your soul will find rest and restoration of all that has been stolen from you.

Lettuce

WEEK

twenty-six

day 176   dream

Babies sleep a lot at this point in development. Their deepest sleep is called REM sleep, short for rapid eye movement; this is when they dream. Can you imagine what your baby could be dreaming about? Dreams are often dismissed as the result of the spicy food or pizza you had for dinner. Maybe that's true. But dreams can also be an avenue God uses to speak to you. He spoke to people through dreams in biblical times, giving warnings and directions for their lives. Pray today for both the literal and spiritual dreams He will give your child.

Praise the Lord for promising to pour out His Spirit on all flesh, when sons and daughters will prophesy and young men will see visions (Acts 2:17).

Pray God will open the spiritual ears of your child as they sleep (Job 38:14–15).

Ask God to plant His dreams in your child's heart to see His will advance on the earth.

Momma,

Do you dream when you sleep? Consider the many times God spoke through dreams—to Joseph, Nebuchadnezzar, Daniel, and Mary's fiancé, Joseph. He gave them specific details and directions for their safety and future. So why does He speak this way? Often, when you're awake, you don't easily hear God's voice. Dreams can appear so real that your senses are heavily impacted. Take notice of your dreams. Maybe keep a journal if you're having a recurring dream or theme. God could be trying to get your attention or highlight an issue you've not considered before. He loves to teach you new ways of receiving from Him. Don't limit the limitless God.

day 177 faith

Your baby's living quarters are dark, and his or her eyes remain closed. God's perfect design shows His glory as He knits babies together perfectly in the unseen place. How He grows your baby from a tiny little embryo to a full baby in just nine months is such a mystery. It is often in the unseen or dark seasons that He produces beauty. These are the times in your life when He establishes faith. Today, pray for your child's faith to be purified in times of testing and trial.

Praise God, who gives salvation through faith alone so no one can boast in their works (Ephesians 2:8-9).

Thank God, who is faithful, that He will establish your child and guard them against the Evil One (2 Thessalonians 3:3).

Pray your little one will take up their shield of faith in all circumstances and quench the fiery darts of the Evil One (Ephesians 6:16).

Momma,

The first chapter of James tells you how to respond to trials by considering facing them with pure joy. How can you possibly do that apart from being fully convinced of God's love for you? Those three faith-filled guys—Shadrach, Meshach, and Abednego—experienced a miraculous manifestation of God's presence in the very fire of their trial. How glorious that these men were not even touched by the flames because the presence of God was so overwhelming. As faith is being built in you, beloved, do not avoid the very way God is going to show you His glory. Long more for His presence to grow in you than for the problem to go away.

day 178 strength

Your baby's muscle tone is beginning to increase. The little muscles will one day provide strength for them to sit up, roll over, and take those first steps. Their muscles also provide shape to their bodies, covering their fragile skeleton. Without them, it would be like living in a house with no walls. God's perfect design for growing His church is through the gifts He gives the body. Spiritual gifts strengthen brothers and sisters, giving support to the whole body.

Today, read 1 Corinthians 12:5-11 and pray for the spiritual gifts God wants to manifest through your child:

> To each is given the manifestation of the Spirit for the common good. For to one is given through the Spirit the utterance of wisdom, and to another the utterance of knowledge according to the same Spirit, to another faith by the same Spirit, to another gifts of healing by the one Spirit, to another the working or miracles, to another prophecy, to another the ability to distinguish between spirits, to another various kinds of tongues, to another the interpretation of tongues. All these are empowered by one and the same Spirit, who apportions to each one individually as he wills.

Momma,

You are uniquely gifted for the kingdom. You give, through the Spirit's help, what no one else on earth can give to the body of Christ. Beloved, you were made to do good, unique works (Ephesians 2:10). You will know you're using that spiritual gift when you experience the joy of the Spirit. You will feel as if it's natural to you. You were made to help build up the body through your gifting. When we all use our gifts and talents, imagine how beautiful and powerful that is.

day 179 authority

Your little one's brain is already directing their tiny eyelids to open, even though they won't yet. All your baby's muscle movement is caused by their brain cells communicating with their nerves. Your own head directs the rest of your body through an intricate system of nerves and muscles. God's design is quite fascinating. As you're praying over your baby today, think of the complex ways God is sovereign over every minute detail in your little one's life. He reigns over both the expanse of creation and carefully attends to every need of your child's life.

Thank God that His ways are higher than our ways. He knows the best way to bring Himself glory (Psalm 115:3). Pray your child will know Him intimately and submit to His lordship.

Rejoice that Jesus has authority over everything: evil, nature, sickness, sin, and humanity (Mark 1:23-27; Matthew 8:14-15; 9:6).

Pray your son or daughter will submit to godly authority willingly and joyfully (Titus 3:1).

Momma,

You are soon entering a new position of authority, parenthood. True authority flows from the heart of God as your Father. False authority is demanding and ungracious. The more you grow in love, the more you grow in authority. He never holds His power and might over His child. He rules with mercy and grace, and He will empower you to lead your child as He leads you. He is the perfect parent and will perfect you as you learn from Him.

day 180 fragrant

Your baby is immersed in a womb full of sensory information, especially smells. They experience some distinction between smells, which is directly connected to tastes. Smelling is powerfully linked to memories, emotions, and pleasures, and it can even be used to warn against danger, such as smoke. God blesses you with the fragrance of a rose or the fresh smell of rain.

As you pray for your baby, pray they grow in discernment.

Pray your son or daughter will spread the fragrance of the knowledge of Christ everywhere (2 Corinthians 2:14).

Praise God for counting your child's prayers as incense before Him (Psalm 141:2).

Pray that your child's memories and associations will be blessed. Spend time thanking God that Christ's blood can heal any sin, trauma, or offense.

Momma,

Your life is a living perfume—to some you smell like the beauty of Jesus. Your presence carries the very essence of heaven. It's Jesus in you. Do you see your life in this way? Every trip to the grocery store or to your job becomes a mini mission trip. As you engage with others, such as the cashier or your coworkers, you will draw others to Him. Your spiritual smell is distinct, and others will notice.

day 181   disciple

Your little one is already smelling and tasting some of what you're eating and drinking. Studies have shown that babies respond to various stimuli, like that cup of coffee you sipped this morning. This is a beautiful picture of how you will model your response to the Lord's leading. As you grow in your relationship with the Lord, your child will also be affected and blessed by the fruit you bear. You will disciple your son or daughter in various ways, such as by teaching, by showing, and by simply abiding in the Lord. You are fulfilling the Great Commission right in your own home.

Pray that as you disciple your child, they will also disciple others in the kingdom of God (Matthew 28:19-20).

Ask that your child will imitate you as you imitate Christ (1 Corinthians 11:1).

Thank the Father for bearing out His image in your son or daughter. Pray they walk in their true identity as God's child.

Momma,

Jesus adores relationship. It's His way of relating to you, beloved. You grow in faith as you spend time talking to Him, listening to Him when He speaks through His Word, and intentionally worshiping Him. He absolutely loves seeing you respond to Him as He draws you through the Spirit. Worshiping God is much more than singing. Worship manifests from a heart set on loving Him. It manifests in many different ways and can be difficult to define. Think of your whole life as worship. What does cooking dinner or taking a relaxing walk look like? Ask Him today how He wants you to worship Him.

day 182 — life

Your baby's blood continues to transport nutrients to his or her body through both the umbilical cord and placenta. Blood is the life source of the whole body. It acts like a conveyer belt, carrying oxygen, nutrients, and even waste to their proper places. Where there's no blood, there's no life. As you pray today, consider Jesus's blood and its power in your child's life as the vital life-giving source of forgiveness, healing, and redemption. Nothing is more powerful than the blood of Christ.

Praise the Lord for reconciling your child to Him, making peace with them by His blood (Colossians 1:20).

Thank Jesus for shedding His blood on the cross to cover and cleanse your child's sin (Hebrews 9:22).

Pray that your son or daughter will pray with confidence and draw near to the Father with a true heart and full assurance made possible through the blood of Jesus (Hebrews 10:19-22).

Momma,

Be blessed with the truth and freedom found in these lyrics from the hymn "There Is Power in the Blood." Amen.

Would you be free from the burden of sin?
There's pow'r in the blood, pow'r in the blood;
Would you o'er evil a victory win?
There's wonderful pow'r in the blood.
There is pow'r, pow'r, wonder-working pow'r
In the blood of the Lamb;
There is pow'r, pow'r, wonder-working pow'r
In the precious blood of the Lamb.
—Lewis E. Jones, One Lord, One Faith, One Baptism: an African American ecumenical hymnal, #375 (1899)

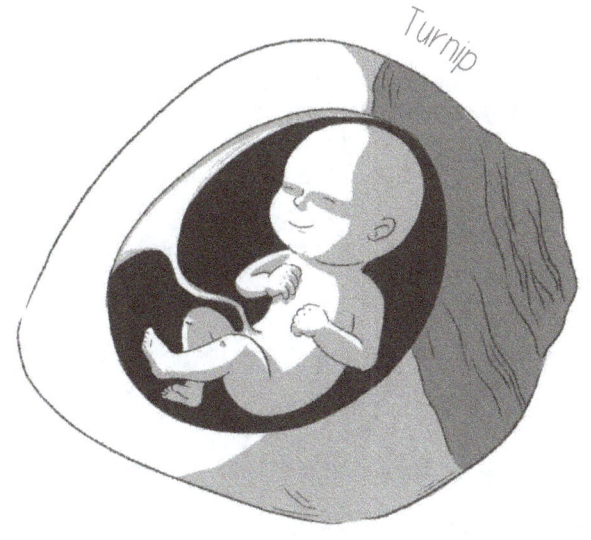

Turnip

WEEK

twenty-seven

day 183 confess

Your baby has begun to expel tiny amounts of urine or liquid waste into their amniotic fluid. As your little one reaches full term, getting rid of waste will increase. The way God designed your baby's body to stay healthy by ridding itself of unwanted and unneeded waste is a perfect picture of confession. Confessing sin to the Lord purges your soul of waste. As you consider confession today, pray your child will live a lifestyle of repentance.

Thank God for the grace He gives your son or daughter as they confess their sin. He promises to freely forgive them and cleanse them of all unrighteousness (1 John 1:9).

Pray the Father will gently remove spiritual logs from your child's vision so he or she can see clearly. Then your child will be able to deal with the speck in another's eye (Matthew 7:5).

Momma,

Do you want to hear what freedom for your heart sounds like? Freedom is this: you no longer have to deal with your sin. Jesus already dealt with it on the cross. The power sin had in your life has been completely broken, and now you're free to live in the abundant life of Christ. Second Corinthians 5:21 says Jesus became sin so you could become the righteousness of God. By faith, believe His Word and promise to you. Turn your eyes from the sinful habits in your life, and look to Jesus and what He did for you. Take heart, you're becoming everything He paid for.

day 184 resurrection

Take heart, Momma. Soon you will see that little face you've been praying for. The bones are continuing to harden and be strengthened. The skeleton is important, as it gives shape and structure to the entire body. Walking, standing, bending, and other physical activities wouldn't be possible without strong bones. Today, as you pray for your child, ask that God grant them a strong faith. All other virtues will flow from faith, including love, prayer, and life in Christ. Everything builds on the foundation of believing in and trusting God.

Read the account of the valley of dry bones in Ezekiel 37:1-14. Thank the Lord for the glorious way He breathes His Spirit over dry bones and brings them to life. He raises them up for new purposes. He takes scattered bones and builds a fortified army. What seemed dead and impossible has been met with the miracle-restoring hand of God. What may seem impossible for your child may be also met with divine help from heaven (Luke 1:37).

Momma,

Jesus is drawn to your faith. He wants you to believe the Father the way He did. He had trials on earth just like you, but He was never moved by the circumstances. He knew His purpose, so He was not overwhelmed by life. If you're called to be like Him on the earth, you might wonder why you are tempted to be consumed by the cares of this life. Know why you wake up in the morning. It cannot be to work a job, mother a child, or finish your education. Your reason is to live and become as Jesus, glorifying Him **while** you work your job, mother a child, and finish your education.

day 185 resemblance

Your baby's tiny face is almost fully formed with eyebrows, hair, and white eyelashes. Their eyelashes and hair are white at the moment because their pigment, or color, hasn't developed yet. By the time they are born, pigment will be added, even if it's not their permanent hair hue. Genetics play a major role in hair color, with brown and black hair being dominant over lighter colors like blonde or red. God's design is that your child look like their parents. As you pray, ask that your little one will resemble His spiritual DNA by bearing out the image of Christ.

Pray that your child will abide in Christ, walking the same way Jesus walked (1 John 2:6).

Ask that God give your little one a life worth imitating (1 Corinthians 11:1).

Praise God that He foreknew your baby, desiring them to be conformed to the image of Jesus (Romans 8:29).

Momma,

Do you live in the reality that God intimately knows you? He has planted you exactly where He desires, and all your circumstances are perfect for molding you into the image of Jesus. He doesn't waste a thing. Nothing. Begin to believe Him for how He is shaping you. Shine brightly in the midst of all situations, bearing out the beautiful life of Jesus. The world is watching, and they are hungry for the hope He alone can give (Matthew 5:14-16).

day 186   abide

At this stage, your baby has begun to fill out and gain weight, transforming their wrinkled, dimpled look into a round little bundle of joy. While too much weight is unhealthy, their little body was designed to maintain fat for energy production and temperature regulation. Little ones are naturally drawn to sweet foods, but too much sugar can be harmful. Pray God will give you wisdom as you choose the meals and snacks you will give your baby. A diet of fruits and vegetables will ensure your little one will maintain a healthy weight and establish good eating habits for life.

Praise the Lord, who promises that as your child loves God and is called according to His purpose, He will work everything together for their good (Romans 8:28-29). God will use all things to conform your child into the image of Jesus.

Thank the Lord for desiring to fill and empower your child to walk according to the Word and know how to discern between evil and good (Hebrews 5:14).

Pray your child will live, move, and have their being in Christ (Acts 17:28).

Momma,

What does it mean to live and move and have your being in Christ? It is a life fully submitted to the Spirit, manifesting the life of Jesus. He spoke only what the Father spoke and did only the works He saw Him doing (John 5:19). Have you come to the end of yourself, desiring to crucify your natural reasoning and thoughts to have the mind of Christ alone? All of the fruit of the Spirit is produced by abiding (John 15:5). Abiding is intentional but not dutiful. Stay attached to the Vine, drawing from His ever-giving life.

day 187 — hear

According to studies, your baby can now distinguish sounds outside your womb, such as voices and music. If you've been gabbing away to your little one or playing them your favorite soundtrack, you're not being silly. They are listening. As you pray today, thank God for the gift of hearing. Your child will can recognize your voice more often, distinguishing it from all others. Pray your child will obey and heed your direction, which leads to blessing in their life.

Praise the Lord for speaking to your child's heart. As He speaks, pray your little one will have ears to hear and a heart to understand spiritual truth (Mark 4:23).

Thank God for His patience as He teaches your child to recognize His voice. This process can take years, but God is always willing to wait on His children (Isaiah 30:18).

Praise the Father for His Word that never returns empty. As your little one dwells in Christ and in God's Word, they can ask anything and God will answer (John 15:16).

Momma,

You know the difference between hearing and obeying. When you hear God's Word, your heart may be stirred and touched, producing faith. But faith without works is dead (James 2:17-18). God speaks so you can obey by faith what He is directing. Let everything you do be motivated by love, and when it's not, confess it to Him. Beloved, He has already forgiven you. You're acknowledging and receiving the grace He has already paid for on the cross. Your obedience will become effortless as you trust His love.

day 188   holy

Your womb has become a symphony hall, full of sounds and vibrations that your baby may remember when they are born. Babies learn the language you speak to them. Your baby will one day become a little child who mimics your words and attitudes. How does that change the way you live now? You will make choices for everything your child will be engaged with—cartoons, music, social media, friendships. Your hope in modeling Christlikeness is that one day your child will grow in making their own decisions about holiness. Pray today that your little one will be holy and set apart from their generation.

Pray your child will purify themself of everything that contaminates their body and spirit and that they will be complete in holiness (2 Corinthians 7:1).

Bless your child with purity, asking that they live according to God's Word (Psalm 119:9).

Pray that your son or daughter offers up their body as a living sacrifice, holy and pleasing to the Lord (Romans 12:1).

Momma,

God's Word says to **be** holy, not just to do holy things (1 Peter 1:15–16). It's easy to appear good and upright while your heart is full of impurity. You can go to Bible studies, attend church regularly, hold your tongue, and delete that angry text message before sending it. But God's not after your behavior. He is supremely after your heart. You will do holy things because He has made you holy. When you believe His blood gives you peace with Him, you will come to know who you truly are as His daughter. Then the doing will flow from a heart made right.

day 189 remember

Did you know your little one prefers your voice over others? Studies show that your "motherese" or high-pitched baby talk is a comfort to your baby. They can remember your voice because it is permanently wired into their little brain for the rest of their life. Their earliest memories will be forever connected to childhood. First schoolday, the first time riding a bike, and even learning how food tastes are all linked into memory. Pray today that your little one will remember the goodness of God in all things.

Praise the Lord for promising not to remember your child's sins by forever blotting them out by His blood (Isaiah 43:25).

Thank the Lord for remembering that you are as dust (Psalm 103:14) and for keeping no record of wrongs (1 Corinthians 13:5).

Pray your son or daughter will forget "the former things" (Isaiah 43:18), not look back regretfully, and always press on to what God is doing now and in the future.

Momma,

Sit. Breathe. Relax. Meditate. Begin to think of God's kindness and provision in your life. Set your mind to remembering His healings, His deliverances, His victories, and His discipline. All of it has been good because He is good and works all things together for your good (Romans 8:28). As you recall who He has been for you, you will sense your faith being strengthened for this day and the days ahead. He's never failed you, left you, or unloved you, and He won't start now. Jesus Christ is the same today, yesterday, and forever (Hebrews 13:8).

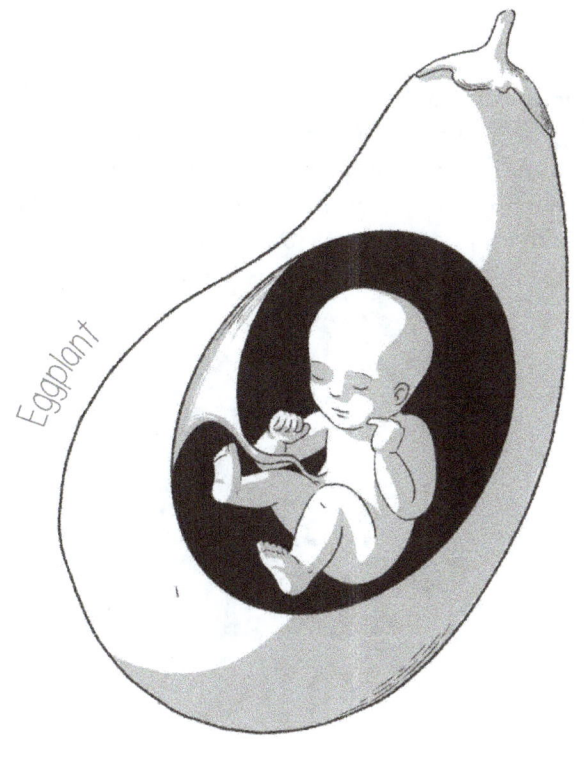

Eggplant

WEEK

twenty-eight

day 190 ~ breathe

Your little one is practicing for his or her grand entrance into the world of breathing oxygen. Miraculously, your baby breathes in amniotic fluid while swallowing a small amount. Breathing is obviously essential for life; it can be shallow, rapid, and affected by various things, but without breath, there can be no life. God first breathed into man and sustains every human life with His gracious breath.

Pray your little one will live by Scripture, which contains the very words breathed by God (2 Timothy 3:16).

Ask the Father to give your child a revelation of eternity and an eternal perspective. Pray that your son or daughter will know their life is fleeting (Psalm 144:4).

Pray your little one will use their breath to praise the Lord (Psalm 150:6).

Momma,

Where do you need the Lord to come and blow refreshing life? He is an expert at reviving dead marriages, people, and situations. He blows His breath of hope into your soul, and all of a sudden, the impossible becomes possible. Some areas of your heart may have grown stale and stagnant. He knows it already, beloved. He longs to give you a fresh vibrancy that energizes you with faith. Sing the lyrics: ""Breathe on me, Breath of God, / Fill me with life anew, / That I may love the way you love, / And do what you would do." (Edwin Hatch, "Breathe on Me, Breath of God.?" (1878))

day 191 purify

Your baby's ability to detect pain and pressure, especially in the fingertips, is still developing. Their nervous system is still immature and the experience of pain is very different from that of a newborn or adult, but it exists. Pain is a good signal for alerting your body to a problem. Sometimes, these pains will alert your child to confess sin and other pains will be because of the sin of others. All of it will be used to purify the heart of your son or daughter.

Pray your child will consider it joy when he or she meets trials of various kinds, knowing that the testing of his or her faith will produce steadfastness (James 1:2-3).

Thank God for blessing your child as he or she remains steadfast under trial. God promises to bless him or her with a crown of life (James 1:12).

Pray your son or daughter will rejoice in trial knowing that realness, or genuineness, of his or her faith will be revealed (1 Peter 1:6-7).

Momma,

Consider your current trials. How are you responding? If your default is anything less than rest and peace, you're in a perfect place to grow. The fruit of the Spirit grows in the soil of adversity. It softens and refines us, conforming us more into the image of love, joy, peace, patience, kindness, goodness, faithfulness, gentleness, and self-control (Galatians 5:22-23). God isn't after flaky, flighty faith. He wants it to be genuine and pure, as He is genuine and pure. Thank Him for empowering you to grow in the soil of trials. You will see the most beautiful harvest as He waters you with His Spirit.

day 192   grace

Today, your baby's largest organ—the skin—is complete and contains sweat glands. Amazing, right? Although your little one won't need it now, sweat is produced through physical exercise and heat to help cool the body down from dangerous temperatures. God's perfect design created a method for relief. As you're thinking about your baby's sweat glands, consider the pressures she or he will experience in life. Thank God for the times of spiritual sweating, when your son or daughter will know the ever-present grace of God.

Thank God for the sufficient grace He gives for every need concerning your child (2 Corinthians 12:9).

Praise Jesus for experiencing internal wrestling, even sweating drops of blood in the garden before His crucifixion (Luke 22:44). He already bore all the stress your child would ever face. He even promised trouble in this life but added that He has overcome the world (John 16:33). Pray your child will know the overcoming life of Christ.

Momma,

Did you ever think you would thank God for the gift of sweating? May your heart well up in praise for the intimate way He has made such perfect provisions, often ones you might take for granted. Sweating, though unpleasant, is actually a gift. Begin to see your tests in this way. They're not pleasant, but in Christ you can shine in the midst of them. Your Father doesn't waste anything. He is working all things together for your good (Romans 8:28). How does this give you fresh spiritual eyes about your trials?

day 193 touch

What a sweet thought to know your baby can actually sneeze already. Their skin is also sensitive and will respond now to touch. You're eager to touch your baby, and those first touches are crucial to life, especially for a newborn. The first time you hold your baby, you will probably examine his or her tiny toes and fingers with joy, staring at your miracle for hours. Today, pray your child will respond eagerly to the touch of the Spirit as He draws them for salvation. You are simply praying the Father's will; He loves bringing another child into His kingdom.

Praise God for the way He will touch your child's heart, uniquely and exclusively (1 Samuel 10:26).

Rejoice in the Lord because He protects your child so the Evil One will not touch them (1 John 5:18). Rest in this promise.

Thank Jesus for His healing touch in your child's life (Luke 18:15). Pray your son or daughter will walk in the power of praying for healing, to God's glory.

Momma,

Let Jesus press in and gently touch your soul. Allow His hand to touch your heart, restoring all the broken places. The words to the hymn "The Touch of His Hand on Mine," written by Jessie Brown Pounds in 1913, proclaims God's ability to be all you need:

Oh, the touch of His hand on mine,
Oh, the touch of His hand on mine!
There is grace and pow'r, in the trying hour,
In the touch of His hand on mine.

day 194 comfort

Your little one is an amazing learner already. He or she can respond by sucking when something familiar is said. If you read to your baby, studies show he or she will recognize your voice after birth. That's amazing! Familiarity is a key to comfort. Pray Jesus will become your son or daughter's refuge when they seek to be comforted in times of grief and testing.

Pray your child will intimately know the God of all comfort in times of affliction (2 Corinthians 1:3-4).

Ask for your son or daughter to find comfort in God's Word and His discipline (Psalm 23:4).

Rejoice that your child will experience in trial the closeness of God, who promises to be close to the brokenhearted (Psalm 34:18).

Momma,

Where do you turn for deep, heart-level comfort? Jesus tells you to come to Him for rest (Matthew 11:28). Your weary heart is safe in His hands. He will often sit with you in your test, giving you grace hour by hour (2 Corinthians 12:9). He longs for you to know His presence, and if you miss His presence in the midst of the trial, you've missed His purpose. Begin to recognize Him behind every friendly smile, every word of comfort, every act of solace or sympathy. It's Him. He is working through those people and things to attract your gaze. He loves you that much, beloved.

day 195   dwell

Your little one's ability to remember what you read and say is directly linked to the sucking reflex. For example, if you read the same book over nine months of pregnancy, those same words will be familiar to him or her after birth. Pray that as your child grows, they will hide God's Word in their heart. The truths of Scripture will manifest in wisdom, peace, and abundant life as your little one obeys God.

Pray your child will hide God's Word in their heart so they will not sin against God (Psalm 119:11).

Pray the Word of Christ will dwell richly in your son or daughter with all wisdom (Colossians 3:16).

Ask that your child will abide in Jesus and Jesus's words abide in them (John 15:7).

Pray your child will hold fast to the Word of Life (Philippians 2:16).

Ask that your son or daughter will walk by the Word of God and know its power for a Spirit-filled life (Deuteronomy 8).

Momma,

The Word of God is a two-edged sword, living and active (Hebrews 4:12). Jesus is the Word, and His truth cuts to the very heart of your life. His Word has to renew your mind, or else you will live according to your natural, fleshly reasoning. You were not meant to live like Adam, but like Christ. You were literally given the mind of Christ (1 Corinthians 2:16). As the Holy Spirit draws you to sit with Him awhile, let His Word challenge you. Let Him give you His perspective so you can be forever changed into His likeness.

day 196 position

While you may feel as if your baby is doing somersaults in your womb, he or she will soon be snuggled head down in your cervix. Your little one is getting into position before birth, so hang in there if it feels like he or she loves being under your ribs. Spiritually, consider where God has placed your son or daughter in His kingdom. God is Father to many children; He loves to place His kids in specific places at specific times for His specific purpose. Nothing is a coincidence or accident. Today, rejoice that your baby is perfectly placed in this generation as part of God's beautiful plan.

Praise the Lord for desiring to raise your child up to heavenly places in Christ Jesus (Ephesians 2:6).

Thank God, who hides your child in Christ Jesus at salvation (Colossians 3:3).

Praise Jesus for going into heaven and sitting at the right hand of the Father and that the angels, authorities, and powers are subject to Him (1 Peter 3:22).

Momma,

Jesus adores taking the small and despised things of the world and bringing Himself glory through them. Your life, beloved, is among His favorite things to show and tell. In fact, angels long to look into the grace God has lavished on you (1 Peter 1:12). They peek into your life, and while you may perceive it to be insignificant and unnoticed, these divine beings marvel at you. Can you imagine the heavenly host eagerly watching you with their jaws dropped wide open?

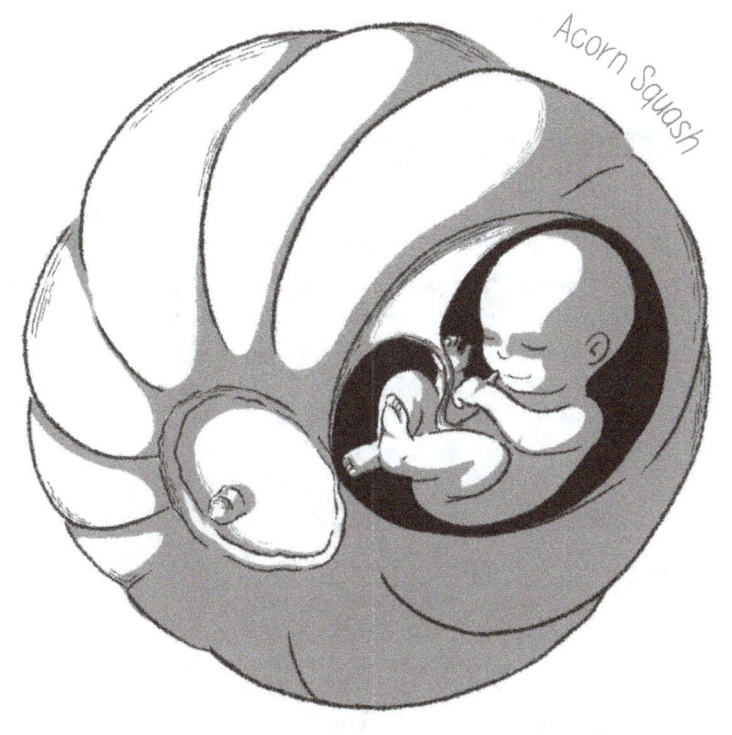

Acorn Squash

WEEK

twenty-nine

day 197 paradox

You may be carrying twins, and if so, each baby could be positioned the exact opposite of the other in your belly. Twins can look exactly alike if they are identical, while fraternal twins do not. You will still be buying two of everything and having twice as much fun, of course. Just as your twins will be settled in opposite directions, consider the kingdom of God, which operates on paradoxes: dying means finding true life, giving is better than receiving, and becoming last means you will be elevated to first place. Pray your son or daughter will know and walk in a kingdom worldview and become a servant to all.

Pray your child embraces death to self as their only way to true joy in Jesus (Luke 9:23).

Pray your son or daughter will humbly walk in the way of Jesus and put themself last (Matthew 20:16).

Ask God to give your little one a servant's heart and put the needs of others before their own (Philippians 2:3).

Momma,

You are about to dive headfirst into a lifestyle of service with your baby. God is going to teach you daily and hourly about giving, loving, and serving your child while denying yourself sleep and energy. You will experience washing your little one's feet spiritually as you perform everyday, mundane tasks with grace. When you are tempted to put your eyes on yourself and grumble or if you feel overwhelmed, Jesus promises rest. His kingdom operates in rest, while the world operates in work. To do more, God wants you to sit in His presence, and in doing so, He will multiply your productivity.

day 198 imitate

Your baby is already learning your distinct voice. He or she is memorizing the unique sound of Momma's tone. He or she will discern what you're saying and how you're saying it. Pray your child will imitate your life in Christ. They will see you responding by being patient and gentle, full of forgiveness, love, and mercy in all circumstances. And even when you sin, your little one will see you walk in grace. Your child will come to learn the Christ-life by watching you.

Ask God to give your little one a heart and eyes to imitate your life in Christ (1 Corinthians 11:1).

Pray your son or daughter will follow and imitate God in everything they do (Ephesians 5:1).

Ask the Lord to give your child godly examples in the body of Christ for them to imitate (2 Thessalonians 3:7).

Momma,

After reading and praying over today's entry, do not let expectations of yourself paralyze you. You are going to be a wonderful parent because God is the best parent. He will give you little tests along the way. Some you will pass the first time; others you will need to take again and again. But He will make sure you're equipped with His promises and will ensure you master every lesson. His grace is sufficient, beloved.

day 199 language

Your baby's ability to connect with you and others depends on the language he or she heard in your womb. If you speak English with a Southern accent, your little one will speak that way too. Language is essential for communicating and takes on many forms, including words that are spoken, written, signed, or expressed with your body. As your son or daughter grow, pray that they will learn the language of heaven. The language of the world is sin, heartache, anxiety, and fear. The language of heaven is grace, forgiveness, mercy, and love.

Praise Jesus for ransoming people from every tribe, language, and nation (Revelation 5:9). He longs to save your child so they can be on a mission everywhere they go.

Pray your child will speak with the tongues of angels and men, manifesting love (1 Corinthians 13:1).

Ask God to grant your child speech that always ministers grace to those listening to them (Colossians 4:6).

Momma,

If you quiet yourself and be still, you will start to hear the language of God. It's simple and filled with peace and love. When the Father speaks to you, even when He is correcting you, He is gentle. He desires to take your mouth and fill it with language that defies boundaries: the language of the heart. It can be understood even when it's not spoken aloud. Your soul needs to rest in the communication of heaven, which is God's Word. Every spoken promise is yours. Will you simply believe?

day 200 precious

You're probably noticing a small belly bump, or if you're having baby number two (or more), your bump may be larger more quickly this time around. Your doctor will check you regularly to ensure your weight gain stays at a healthy pace for the next several months. The pounds you put on will be mostly baby and fluid, and with the proper diet and exercise, you can shed that weight after your little one arrives.

Today's prayers focus on you, Momma. You may be tempted to feel self-conscious during or after your pregnancy. Because of hormonal changes, your skin and hair may be different. Your mood and emotions will fluctuate. Your mirror may be a place of being self-criticism, but looks at your heart. As you seek to beautify your heart, your face and attitude will reflect Jesus. Obsess about God's thoughts toward you.

Meditate on 1 Samuel 16:7: "Do not look on his appearance or on the height of his stature, because I have rejected him. For the LORD sees not as man sees: man looks on the outward appearance, but the LORD looks on the heart."

"Let your adorning be the hidden person of the heart with the imperishable beauty of a gentle and quiet spirit, which in God's sight is very precious" (1 Peter 3:3–4).

Momma,

Being a woman seems to automatically come attached with the desire to be beautiful. The world wants to redefine what true beauty is, so we have to lean into truth when we feel tempted to judge our appearance. Jesus was not particularly special looking (Isaiah 53:2), yet His heart of love was the most appealing thing about Him. It makes Him irresistible to others. Today, ask Him to make your heart the most beautiful aspect of your appearance. He is living inside you, so you are already beautiful!

day 207 fruit-bearer

Babies can show certain likes and preferences. When they are given sweet foods, babies might manifest contentment, but for sour and salty foods, they may turn their faces away. Spiritually, your son or daughter will have choices to make in life. Your prayers now can call down blessings over your child's life, especially in times of testing and trial. Ask for your child to make godly, wise decisions. Intercede for sweet fruit to bear out in love, joy, and peace (Galatians 5:22).

Pray your son or daughter will bear the fruit of righteousness springing up into a tree of life (Proverbs 11:30).

Jesus's desire for your child is for them to have fruit that remains, not ever rotting or fading like the fruit of the world. Pray your child will abide in Jesus, the Vine, and bear out the Christ-life (John 15:1-5, 16).

Pray for your child to have a repentant heart, allowing the Holy Spirit to prune away the sinful places so even more fruit can be produced (Matthew 3:8).

Momma,

Simply put, your baby is a seed-bearing fruit of your womb who carries the seed for future generations of other seed bearers. The design of the Father is beautiful: He places His image on every human. The fruit of His Spirit takes time to be cultivated in the soil of your heart. He fertilizes it with His Word and showers it with His living water. Today, consider praying for your family, your future children, your grandchildren, and your spiritual heritage (Deuteronomy 7:9). What can you dream for your legacy, beloved?

day 202   joy

Your baby can flash a precious grin already—their little smiles can be captured on an ultrasound picture. What could possibly make your baby smile in the womb? Although that's a mystery for now, you know smiling is an expression of happiness and joy. Today, as you are praying, ask God for the fruit of joy to be deeply planted into the heart of your son or daughter. Pray they will be a cheerful giver, delighted in the Lord and His ways.

Pray your child will rejoice always, pray constantly, and give thanks in all circumstances, knowing this is God's will (1 Thessalonians 5:16-18).

Ask the Spirit to express His full joy through your child (Galatians 5:22; John 15:11).

Pray the joy of the Lord will be your son or daughter's strength (Nehemiah 8:10).

Momma,

You will discover the joy of your heavenly Father as you raise this baby. The way He rejoices over you will be reflected in the way you take joy in your child. A parent's joy is not dependent on behavior but is rooted in relationship. Even when your little one sins, your joy is maintained by simply being their parent. During those hard days and long nights with your baby, you can cling to the promise that joy comes in the morning.

day 203 rest

Your little one is maturing and growing every single day. While he or she seems to be moving constantly, you may notice more spurts of rest. God purposely designed you to need rest, both spiritually and physically. Learning to rest in the Lord is a mark of maturing in Him. Your peace will flow from a place of abiding in His love. Pray that your child will live in the rest of God.

Jesus died to purchase an eternal Sabbath rest for your child. Pray they will know and live from this place of rest (Hebrews 4:9).

Pray your child will manifest rest in the Lord so that those who are heavy-laden by life will seek the true giver of rest (Matthew 11:28).

Pray for your son or daughter to seek the path of the righteous so they find rest for their soul (Jeremiah 6:16).

Momma,

The world defines your worth by your education and status, how busy you are, where you vacation, how you raise your kids, and how many people you know. But God's kingdom operates on another paradigm (and it's why I am so drawn to its freedom). To rest in Christ and His work on the cross frees you from self-imposed legalism. To be known by Him frees you from making sure your voice is heard among a million others. Rest comes with you deciding that circumstances will not determine your joy because Jesus is your source of joy, and He never changes (Hebrews 13:8), so your joy never changes.

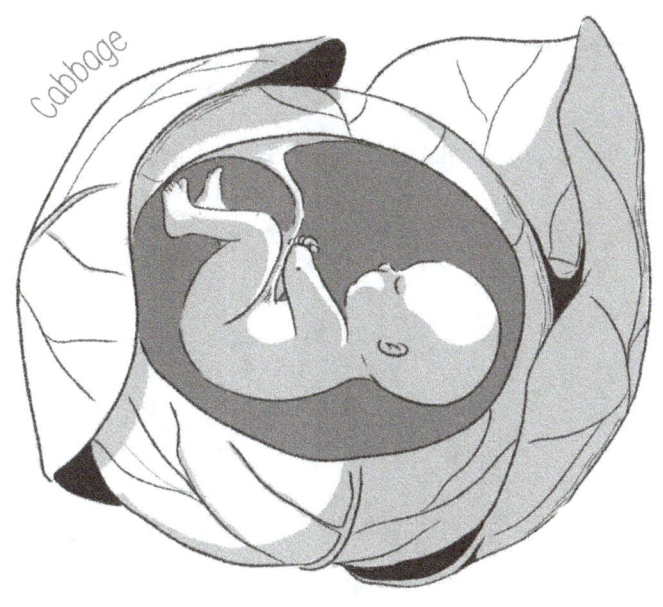

Cabbage

WEEK

thirty

day 204 dreamer

You may have noticed an increase in dreaming at night. While science and the world attribute much of your dreams to hormones or even spicy food before bed, the Lord could be speaking to you in this unique way. Ask Him if there's any significance to your dreams; He may want to give you direction or insight into His heart. He may warn you or home in on a detail of your life that He wants to bring to the surface. Often when you're asleep, God has your full attention, which is why He uses emotion to make your dreams seem so real.

Pray this: Lord, thank You that You are a revealer of mysteries, riddles, and deep things (Daniel 2:47). You speak to me in a vision of the night, and my spirit is fully awake to you while I sleep. Open my heart and mind to receive Your divine messages. I praise You for the dreams You have for my life. I stand in awe of the way You reveal Your goodness to me in the land of the living (Psalm 23:6; 27:13). Thank You, Father, for not limiting the way You want to communicate with Your daughter. Help me to believe You for my literal and figurative dreams. Where there has been a lack of dreaming about Your plans for my life, I thank You for restoring a double portion of faith. I want to believe Your promise to me that You have good plans, a hope, and a future for me (Jeremiah 29:11). I receive Your dreams for my life. I love You, my dreamer God. Have Your way in my life. In Jesus's name, amen.

Momma,

What is the dream of your heart for your child? You may have never thought beyond them having a "good life." God has plans in His mind about your little one (Jeremiah 29:11), and He often uses parents' prayers to call the purposes forth on earth. Begin to ask Him how He specifically wants to fulfill His glory through your child. Pray with joyful expectation!

day 205 light

Your baby can see light when it is shined on your belly. The light is greatly dulled, but it can still be bright enough to catch your little one's attention. What a beautiful picture of the gospel. Your little one is drawn to the light. As you pray, ask for Jesus to shine on your son or daughter's heart. He is the light of the world, and He makes His children shine as brightly as He does.

Praise Jesus for shining His light in the dark places, not ever being overcome by it (John 1:5).

Thank God that your child will follow the light of Jesus and never walk in darkness but will always be lit up with the life of Christ (John 8:32).

Pray your son or daughter will love God's Word and always use it as a lamp to their feet and a light for their path (Psalm 119:105).

Call down the good works the Lord has planned for your child, knowing that others will see them and glorify God (Matthew 5:16).

Momma,

The radiance of Jesus is so bright that all darkness must flee from His presence. His light will expose places in your heart that need to be exchanged for truth. He does not ever expose sin or weak areas to shame you but rather to show you where He wants you to walk in His righteousness. You don't have to fear what He will show you, beloved. That is the very place He will bless you with freedom.

day 206 provision

Your little one is shrouded in your dark womb, but the Lord gives babies a visual function that, once they are born, allows their eyes to adjust quickly to the new, bright world outside. When your child comes to Jesus for salvation, He has everything in place for your child to live a brilliant new life in Him. The Holy Spirit will make adjustments in the spiritual vision of your son or daughter. They will see everything through the eyes of the Spirit.

Thank the Father for rescuing your child from the domain of darkness and bringing them into the kingdom of His Son (Colossians 1:13).

Praise the Father for giving His Spirit, who will be your son or daughter's helper and teacher as they grow in Christ (John 14:16-17, 26).

Thank God, who gave your child everything they need for living a godly life and granted them precious promises (2 Peter 1:3).

Momma,

Today, you lack nothing.

You have everything in Christ to live in this world but not be of it. He is in you and you in Him (John 15:4-5), never to separate again. You have all the resources of heaven because you have heaven's greatest resource: Jesus. Praise Him for taking care of your needs: emotionally, spiritually, and physically. He knows the very number of hairs on your head. He has given you His Word, His Spirit, His very life. What do you need from Him today?

day 207

glory

Your little one has both permanent and baby teeth. Teeth are essential for obvious reasons: chewing food, helping with digestion, and speaking properly. In their first year, babies will likely experience teething. Those tiny tooth buds will pop through the tender gums, making you the proudest parent in the world. That milestone will only be rivaled when your child loses that same tooth for the first time.

Praise Jesus for beginning a good work in your son or daughter. He promises to continue His work until it is finally finished on the day Jesus returns (Philippians 1:6).

Pray your little one will flourish and grow in the Lord (Psalm 92:12-14).

Ask for your child to be rooted in Jesus and for their life to be built on Him alone (Colossians 2:6-7).

Momma,

Have you noticed that Jesus designed every living thing to grow? You were not created to be a baby forever but were made to mature into an adult, yet with childlike faith. God shows something unique about Himself in the maturing process. You have the potential to grow in every test, trial, circumstance, and season. Some seasons in your life are short growth spurts while others will be a lifelong growth. God is the Father of time and knows the perfect pace and way to grow you. He says He is not slow (2 Peter 3:9), even though some moments may feel like it. He sees the complete and whole you. He is working every single detail together to bring you to that place of wholeness.

day 208

gift

Your baby will be born with a totally unique personality even though it may be similar to yours. You may notice from birth they are quiet and content or perhaps alert and aware of their surroundings. God has perfectly formed your little one's personality and temperament. They may be very different from their siblings. Some babies are colicky or fussy; don't fear that he or she is a difficult child. Personalities can change as they mature. As you're praying today, thank God for the distinct calling He has on your child for the building up of the kingdom.

Thank God for being the source of all spiritual gifts (1 Corinthians 12:4-11).

Praise the Lord for the gift He has picked especially for your child. Such gifts will encourage the body of Christ (Ephesians 4:11-13) and bring Him much glory (1 Peter 4:10-11).

Pray your child will not elevate the gifts of the Spirit above the Word of God, but will worship in both Spirit and truth (John 4:24).

Momma,

You will have the best time discovering who your child is over the years. Remember that your son or daughter is always in process, growing and changing, and will need lots of shepherding and discipling (sometimes hourly). But every bit of that teaching and modeling will produce a soul that looks like Jesus and walks like He walks (1 John 2:6). If you begin to notice a sin or weak area in your child's heart, pray the opposite spirit into that place. Watch and believe that Jesus will take dominion over those places. He will rule over your child's heart for His glory.

day 209   pure

Your little one will frequently position its hands near its face, specifically near the mouth. Those tiny little hands, drawn high, almost seem like a mask. Spiritually, you can be reminded that covering the mouth can prevent unwanted words from spilling out. Your child will eventually speak, and when they do, pray they will utter pure words from a pure heart.

Pray your child will walk humbly in the way of the Lord, guarding their heart from the world because out of the overflow of the heart, the mouth speaks (Luke 6:45).

James 3 is a wonderful passage to learn about the wisdom of God concerning the tongue. Pray your son or daughter will speak blessings and be quick to listen, slow to speak, and slow to anger.

Ask that God will grant your child gracious words that bless the hearer (Ephesians 4:29).

Momma,

You want so desperately to control your tongue (maybe not?), believing that biting it is the most loving thing to do. The reality of the Christ-life is speaking love from a sincere heart. What good is speaking gracious words to someone when your heart is still ungracious toward them? That's hypocrisy; you cannot control the smallest member of your body. But Jesus says the "love of Christ" controls you (2 Corinthians 5:14). That includes your tongue, beloved. Take today to confess, and then bless Him.

day 270   heart

Your baby's largest organ, the skin, is continuing to grow and develop. In the months ahead, the thin skin will become less transparent. Your son's or daughter's skin will serve many purposes: filtering, sweating, and protecting other vital organs. Spiritually, as your child matures, pray that they are not consumed with the outward appearance of things but rather the inward person of the heart.

First Samuel 16:7 says the Lord does not regard things the way you do, which is typically by the outward flesh. God is more attentive and judges the heart of a person. The inner self controls outward actions.

Pray your child will know that God is primarily after their heart. He does not desire outward, religious actions if a pure heart of love isn't the motivation (Matthew 23:27). He wants a good relationship for His Son: a pure bride for a pure groom.

As God places His desires in the heart of your child, pray they believe the best of others (1 Corinthians 13:7). Pray your child will not regard anyone according to the flesh, but will have spiritual wisdom and grace for all (2 Corinthians 5:16).

Momma,

What a comfort to know that Jesus sees past the way things appear. He alone is your defense and righteousness, purchased for you on the cross. You, beloved, are always seen and known by your Father. And He sees you perfect and whole in His Son. How freeing to know that He does not nitpick your heart or appearance. He loves you, and He likes you. He likes who He is making you into. You are His. And He is yours forever and ever.

Pineapple

WEEK

thirty-one

day 211 gaze

Your baby has desires for certain stimuli, especially your face. Your little one's favorite way to engage you will be by gazing at you. He or she will study your face and expressions. There's a bond happening when you two behold each other. It solidifies your relationship. As you pray today, consider how you are built in faith as you gaze at God. Seeking the face of God will be your son's or daughter's source of strength, hope, and power in life.

Praise God for making His face shine on your child. May He be gracious to them, lifting up His countenance on your little ones. May He give your child peace (Numbers 6:25-26).

Pray your child will seek the Lord, His strength, and His face continually (1 Chronicles 16:11).

Praise Jesus for declaring that your child's angels in heaven continually see the face of the Father (Matthew 18:10).

Momma,

The Father is always drawing you to deeper places of intimacy with Him. He longs to look into your eyes and reveal His love to you. As you behold His face, you will be transformed. You will become as beautiful and glorious as He. But few choose this kind of pressing in. As you gaze into His glory, you will be consumed in Him. Meditate on the lyrics to this hymn:

Turn your eyes upon Jesus
Look full in His wonderful face
And the things of earth will grow strangely dim
In the light of His glory and grace.

day 272 patience

All righty, Momma, you've reached another milestone: you're only eight weeks away from meeting the little life you've been praying for. You're already so in love with your baby. Anticipation is part of the process of waiting. You may feel like eight weeks is an eternity, or it may feel like a day. Let the Lord teach you the fruit of patience as you wait in rest and joy, trusting His perfect timing.

Pray Jesus will bear out His patient life in and through your child (Galatians 5:22).

Ask for your son or daughter to be strengthened with God's glorious power so they will have endurance and patience (Colossians 1:11).

Pray for the greatest in God's royal law—love—to manifest in your child. Ask for them to walk in patient love toward others (1 Corinthians 13:4).

Momma,

When you got dressed this morning, did you put on patience too? The Father longs to clothe you in His tenderhearted mercy, kindness, humility, and patience (Colossians 3:12). He wants to literally cover you in Himself today, beloved. Do not fear patience; pray for more of it. Pure patience will enable you to bear up under any circumstance with grace and gentleness. You will shine in the midst of a hurried, frazzled, and harsh world if you allow the Spirit to bear out patience in you.

What do you need to be patient for currently?

day 213   blessing

Your baby is about eighteen inches long and weighs almost four pounds. While your little one is young, it is important to bless them. Part of blessing your son or daughter is asking God for His plans for your child. Take time today to simply thank Him for His good gift to you. Speak and write blessings over your child. What do you desire to see God manifest in their lives? Who do you envision them to be? Keep these records of blessing because they will serve as promises from the Lord. You will get to see those blessings come to pass with each season. Examples of blessing your child can be found in Deuteronomy 7:13-14; Psalm 127:1-4; 128:1-6; Proverbs 22:6; and Isaiah 54:13.

Pray this scripture over your baby, "You bless the righteous, O LORD; you cover him with favor as with a shield" (Psalm 5:12)."

Momma,

The worship song "The Blessing" can be a powerful anthem to sing over your child and any of your future children. Its lyrics were written from scripture (Numbers 6:24-26). Take time to worship God for the legacy He is creating through your family. You can envision His blessing over your life and generations to come because of the mercy and grace of Jesus. May your heart swell knowing that He is indeed "for you," as the song so powerfully says. You are declaring beautiful truths over your heritage!

day 214 submitted

Your baby is snuggled nicely in your womb right now. Your bump has likely grown to a round belly. While your body is equipped to maintain a healthy temperature, your baby, too, has everything in place to regulate his or her temperature. The Holy Spirit has been given to you to act as a regulator in many ways. He will control the rate at which your child grows spiritually. Pray that your son or daughter receives salvation at a young age. Ask that your child continually be filled with the Spirit and not fulfill the desires of the flesh.

Praise the Lord for His promise that the Evil One cannot touch your child (1 John 5:18).

Pray the Holy Spirit will guide your child's decisions and prevent them from giving in to natural cravings (Galatians 5:16).

Bless your child, asking that God will fill them with an abundance of the fruit of the Spirit: love, joy, peace, patience, kindness, goodness, faithfulness, gentleness, and self-control (Galatians 5:22).

Momma,

Life in the Spirit is simply to walk as Jesus did on the earth. But there's only one way to obtain this: intimacy with Him. There's no substitute, sermon, or supplement that can create intimacy between you and Jesus. Think of conceiving your baby, time alone with a lover, with one exclusive agenda: showing affection, love, and closeness. Let His love draw you into His presence today. Tell Him how much you love Him. Maybe you need to confess that your love has grown cold. He is not disappointed in you, beloved. He already knows the depths of your heart and loves you without conditions.

day 215 wisdom

Your baby's brain is developing. Many parents are already anticipating how intelligent their child will be. You long for assurance that your son or daughter will learn well and be excited to read, write, and enjoy school. God's perfect design of the human brain is unlike that of other creatures; we have the unique ability to reason and make decisions based on a relationship with Him. Pray that as your child grows and matures spiritually, they will make godly decisions. Ask Him to bless your little one with a spirit of wisdom.

Pray that your home and family will always choose the Lord over every worldly temptation (Joshua 24:15), not having your hearts wrapped around trouble, pleasures, or things in the world (1 John 2:15-17).

Ask the Father to grant your son or daughter His wisdom, knowing He will give it abundantly when asked by faith (James 3:17).

Pray for God's wisdom to be deeply planted in your child, and that they will know the wisdom from above is pure, peaceable, considerate, submissive, impartial, and sincere (James 1:5).

Momma,

Jesus is the very wisdom of God. In Him are hidden all the treasures of wisdom and knowledge (Colossians 2:2-3). It's your delight to do the seeking, as for a buried treasure worth more than gold. He will bring the prize of wisdom to light as you search for Him. The decision to walk in wisdom versus foolishness is one that can literally be the difference between life and death. What do you need wisdom for today, beloved? Start with the book of Proverbs for victory in your finances, relationships, and temptation.

day 276 identity

You may be stocking your baby's nursery full of little pink or blue clothes, depending on your little one's gender. It's fun to dream about your sweet prince or princess. Pray that, as your child grows up, they will find their identity in Christ, not in their earthly position, vocation, education, or gender.

Thank Jesus for setting your son or daughter apart, even before the foundation of the earth, to be chosen and adopted as God's child (Ephesians 1:4–5).

Thank God now for this wonderful promise over your little ones: your son or daughter will be a chosen people, a royal priesthood, a holy nation, God's special possession; they will declare praises to Him who called them out of darkness into marvelous light (1 Peter 2:9).

Momma,

Your identity is totally and fully in Christ. Nothing can change that after salvation. What He says about you is the most important thing about you. And He does not change, even if you do. You may be tempted to find some of your identity in being a wife, a mother, and a friend. Sometimes you can become hyperfocused on one of those roles, but God desires you to make every decision based on being His child. You will become free as you live like a much-loved child, resting and trusting in your Father.

day 217 breath

Your little one's lungs are growing, and as his or her birthday approaches, you may notice some changes in your breathing pattern. Breath is essential for all human beings to live and thrive. In the very beginning, God breathed Himself into all humanity. Have you ever considered how the physical world parallels the spiritual world? Just as God breathed life into your child's being, ask that He will breathe His Spirit into your son's or daughter's spirit, causing true life to spring up.

Praise God that He gives Himself to all people, loving them so much that He gave His only precious Son (John 3:16). He gives life and breath to all people (Acts 17:25).

Rejoice in the Holy Spirit, who made your baby and gives him or her life (Job 33:4).

Read Ezekiel 37:1-14, which is about the miracle of the dry bones. The Lord's purpose is to bring life to that which was dead, dry, and hopeless. Pray God will give your child a greater understanding of this reality as he or she matures in the faith.

Momma,

One, two, three. Take a deep breath. Now, breathe out. Do this a few more times. Sit down. Put away the phone. Listen for the Holy Spirit to speak. Linger, and don't rush your time with Him. He knows your agenda better than you. Let His agenda become your priority. What is He speaking into your heart today, beloved?

Kabocha Squash

WEEK

thirty-two

day 278 — resting

Your baby's little heart is growing and maturing each day. At your practitioner visits, you may notice a gradual decrease in your baby's resting heart rate. It's not beating as fast as it once did as his or her birthday approaches. This is due to the heart pushing blood through the body, doing its job already. As you pray today, think about God's rest that has been provided for your little one's spiritual heart. Pray that your son or daughter will walk in this spiritual rest by faith.

Pray your little one will enter into the rest of God (Hebrews 4:11), ceasing from all works-based religion.

Thank Jesus for offering His rest when your child grows weary. He promises to teach your child His rest (Matthew 11:28).

God rested on the seventh day of creation. Pray your child will embrace the rest of God, which imitates Him (Genesis 2:2-3).

Momma,

Since God rested, the question is, do you? He is literally sitting on His throne. He is not panicked, hurried, anxious, or busy. He is running the entire universe far beyond your comprehension. Don't confuse rest with boredom. Rest can be identified as peace. It's operating and drawing from the Christ-life within. He empowers you with rest. When you're resting, there's a quiet stillness. Let Him come teach you about this perfect rest today, beloved.

day 279 marked

Babies are often marked by an unmistakable birthmark somewhere on their body. When your son or daughter is born, you may discover these marks on a leg, an arm, or anywhere else. These physical marks are a beautiful parallel of how God marks you with His signature design. He has marked His children with undeniable love. Pray your child will fully know God's love.

Thank God for His desire to seal and mark your child with His perfect love (Song of Solomon 8:6).

Your son or daughter, after salvation, will be the living expression of the Father's love on the earth (1 John 4:12).

The lost world will know your child is a Christian as they walk in love and unity with other believers, marking them as God's child (John 17).

Momma,

You cannot deny genes and chromosomes. Inevitably you will look like one or both of your parents. Your features may change dramatically from childhood into adulthood, but still the genes will be present and unchanging. As you grow in Christ, you, too, will begin to look like Him. You will be more conformed to His image of love, grace, and forgiveness. You will look like mercy itself. Wow! He is beautiful, and so are you, beloved.

day 220 hungry

You may be surprised to learn that your little one is ingesting small amounts of amniotic fluid, which has been shown to provide nutritional and developmental benefits. If you've heard the phrase "you are what you eat," consider what you're feasting on spiritually. Perhaps you're not ingesting much of the Word or feeding your spirit with prayer. Begin praying now for the spiritual appetite of your child. Ask God to give your son or daughter a hunger and thirst for a relationship with Him.

Pray your child will hunger and thirst for righteousness, trusting He will fill them (Matthew 5:6).

Jesus said He was the Bread of Life, and He promised that anyone who came to Him would never be hungry again (John 6:35). Pray your child will be satisfied in Christ alone.

Ask that your son or daughter seek the spiritual milk of the Word, which will sustain their growth in the LORD (1 Peter 2:2).

Momma,

Are you feeling like you could eat a house these days? Maybe you've noticed some changes in your cravings since you've been pregnant. Hunger is certainly a motivator. You won't satisfy it passively. You're looking for food until that hunger is satisfied. Think of Jesus Himself as the nourishment for your soul, the true source of life. His table is always set, beloved. He is inviting you today to feast on His life until your heart is full.

day 221 free

You learned yesterday that your little one is taking in nutrients from your amniotic fluid, which is essential for growth. Making unhealthy eating choices can have negative effects on your baby's development. Your spiritual life will also have a great impact on your child's life, so "taste and see that the LORD is good!" (Psalm 34:8). Pray to experience the freedom He desires to give you. As you experience this beautiful fullness in Christ, your son or daughter will be drawn to Jesus in you. You will have an abundant overflow of the Spirit-filled life and realize He is yours. You lack nothing when you have Him.

Galatians 5:1 reminds you that He set you free for the purpose of freedom. He only asks you to give up what you were not meant to carry. Pray for understanding of the depths of freedom he has given—in both you and your child.

Momma,

Today, ask God to search your heart. Psalm 19:14 says, "May these words of my mouth and this meditation of my heart be pleasing in your sight, LORD, my Rock and my Redeemer" (NIV). As you open your heart to Him and He gently reveals a wound or an area where hope is not reigning, confess it before Him. He already knows, beloved. It takes faith to confess sin. He is your heavenly Father, who doesn't dwell on your sin but rather longs to give you freedom through the life of His Son. If you confess doubt, He gives you faith. If you confess impatience, He gives you love. If you confess bitterness, He longs to give you grace and forgiveness.

day 222 ready

You may have experienced a slight tightening of your tummy muscles recently, called Braxton-Hicks contractions. (Contact your practitioner if your contractions are painful.) These minor sensations are simply God's way of preparing your body for your baby's birthday. In the same way your body is prepping, pray the Lord will prepare the soil of your child's heart to receive the seed of the kingdom of heaven. Pray the Holy Spirit will water and fertilize that seed, causing it to grow and flourish.

Pray your child will have spiritual ears to hear the Holy Spirit and believe Him through faith (Revelation 3:22).

Ask the Father to condition the soil of your child's heart, break up the hard ground, and make it fertile and ready to receive His Word (Hosea 10:12).

Thank God for drawing near to your child as they draw near to Him (James 4:8).

Momma,

How much glory does it bring your Father when you walk in the good things He has prepared for you? These good works are custom fit, not to be compared to or rivaled by another. Ephesians 2:10 says these good works have been "prepared beforehand," which means they are already there for you. He has a purpose and a plan that you get to fulfill here on the earth. Seek His heart today. Ask Him where He wants to partner with you in these good works.

Where do you sense Him leading? Journal what's in your heart and how He is speaking to you.

day 223   bond

You may be considering your feeding options by now. Will you breastfeed or bottle-feed? While you are weighing the pros and cons of each option, consider that nursing your baby will give quite a bonding experience. Even with bottle feeding, that will be a time to slow down and look into the eyes of your baby. Bonds being established in your relationship are taking place right now, even before you can see your baby face-to-face. Pray for a Spirit-filled relationship with your child, one built on trust and obedience. Nothing glorifies Christ more than trust and surrender.

Jesus said, "If you love me, you will keep my commandments" (John 14:15). He was speaking of the bond between obedience and love. Pray your child will love the Lord with all their heart, mind, soul, and strength (Mark 12:30). Obedience will always follow.

Pray a spirit of honor over your child, that they will grow to honor you as a parent (Exodus 20:12) and honor others above themselves (Romans 12:10).

Momma,

Your Father is worthy of all your affection. He deserves honor, and He will cause you to honor your natural parents. Consider your relationship with them today. Even if they are deceased, can you speak a blessing over them? Let the love of Jesus heal you so completely that you can honor them, even if they don't act honorably. God loves to bring beauty from ashes (Isaiah 61:3).

day 224 soul soles

The nerves in your little one's foot are maturing now. You will see him or her spread those tiny toes in response to touch. You will marvel at those teeny feet and toes. Just as your son or daughter will react to those gentle strokes to their feet, pray the Lord will guide their every footstep. Pray the mantle of Joshua (found in the first chapter of Joshua) over your little one.

God says to Joshua, "Every place the sole of your foot will tread upon, I have given you, just as I promised to Moses" (Joshua 1:3). Pray that your child will literally walk by faith everywhere they go (2 Corinthians 5:7).

Thank the Lord that wherever He sends your child, their feet will be dressed in the shoes of the gospel of peace (Ephesians 6:15).

Praise God for His loving protection and provision of your son or daughter wherever they go (Psalm 91; 139).

Momma,

Look down at your feet (if you can see them). Are they tired and swollen? Jesus, beautiful Jesus, came not to be served, but to serve, and He demonstrated His service by washing the swollen, dirty feet of his apostles. He is still washing feet today. He cleanses every part of you: your heart, your mind, your body. Sit in His presence today, and invite Him to wash those places of your dirty heart with no shame. There is no cleanliness like holiness.

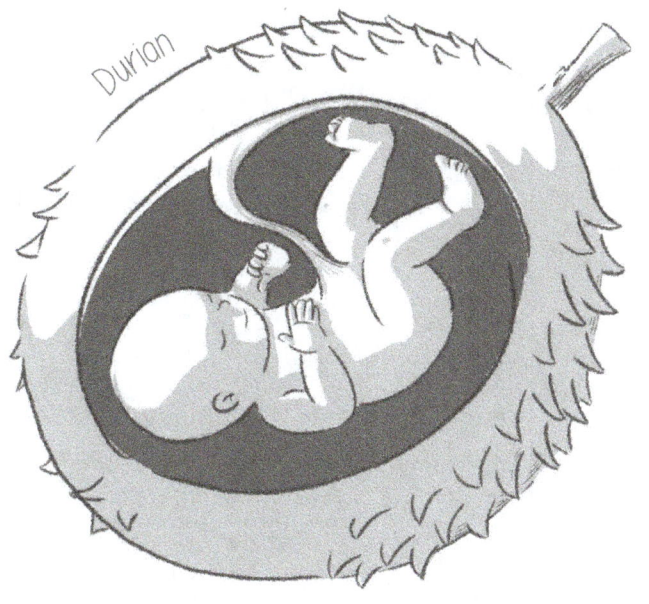

Durian

WEEK

thirty-three

day 225 perceive

Physical eyeballs are obviously for seeing and perceiving the world. All the colors, shapes, and patterns of this life are distinguished through looking and beholding. By looking, your little one will distinguish between a green tree and a blue car. The gift of perception is one of the many aspects of God's creativity. Pray for the spiritual eyes of your child to be opened so they will perceive the work of the Lord in their life.

Pray Ephesians 1:18 over your child, that the eyes of their heart would be enlightened and they would know their calling in Christ.

Pray that your child will pray for others and that through their prayers, others will have their spiritual eyes opened.

Praise the Lord for restoring the spiritual sight to the spiritually blind (Luke 4:18).

Momma,

Consider how many different eye colors there are. Just like we have different eye colors, sometimes your perception, or what you see happening in the natural world, may be skewed based on your experiences and not the truth of God. He desires that you see with His sight. Today, ask God, like Elijah did, "LORD, I pray open my eyes that I may see" (2 Kings 6:17). Immediately you will see His goodness. Ask Him to show you where your spiritual vision needs to be more focused, not skewed or fuzzy.

day 226   heart

Your baby's heart rate should be in the range of 120 to 160 beats per minute. As its little heart develops, pray the Lord will form His will within the heart of your child. Your prayers in this season are especially important because they are the tool used to till and prepare the soil of your child's young heart.

Meditate today on Ezekiel 36:26-27: "I will give you a new heart and... I will put my spirit within you, and cause you to walk in my statutes and be careful to obey my rules."

Do you see all the promises of God in these verses? Thank Him now for what He is going to do in the life of your child. You can begin praying for your son or daughter by inserting their name (unless you haven't decided on a baby name yet) in the following prayer:

Father, You are forming _____'s heart with love and purpose. I pray _____ will walk in Your Spirit, ever listening to Your heartbeat. I thank You for giving _____ a heart of flesh, growing in oneness with You. Teach _____ to guard his [or her] heart because out of it flows the issues of life. May _____ know that You are ever chasing his [or her] heart because You love them and are jealous for them. In the strong name of Jesus, amen.

Momma,

Have you considered personalizing your Bible, inserting your name where promises are given in Scripture? It can be a powerful way to cultivate your relationship with your Father. He knows your name and numbers the very hairs on your head. Find a few verses and plug your name into them, speaking them over yourself in prayer. You can hang them up on your bathroom mirror and put them on your car dash for display. Thank Him for how He is making you like Jesus in every way.

day 227 transform

Those little kicks. You may feel like you're housing a miniature soccer player because of those strong jolts. You also may be experiencing some discomfort if your baby prefers to nuzzle under your ribs. While these minor things will pass soon, remember your response to life comes from the Christ-life within you. Today, as you pray, the focus will be directed within, focused on **your** heart, beloved.

Think on the truth found in Romans 12:2: ""Do not be conformed to this world, but be transformed by the renewal of your mind, that by testing you may discern what is the will of God, what is good and acceptable and perfect." Pray that your child will always know God's will.

Train your mind by thinking His thoughts—by the truth. Jesus promises that the truth will set you free (John 8:32). In every circumstance, ask Him to give you and your child the truth.

Momma,

Jesus says, "Apart from me, you can do nothing" (John 15:5). Lately, maybe you've allowed irritation or frustration to manifest from your heart. He produces the fruit of love, joy, and peace in you. How much better is life in Christ than life apart from Him? Your heart change comes at the moment of confession. Your heart will soften under Jesus's humility and grace. He will remind you of who you truly are: His glory carrier. You glorify Him when you respond to challenges and trials with joy.

Spend time in His Word, seeking His wisdom. Reading the Scriptures alone will not produce fruit that is produced through relationship with Him. Knowing Him, talking with Him, communing with the Spirit, listening, and receiving are all ways you will be changed by His Word. He is the Word (John 1:1).

day 228 remember

You will be amazed to know that, shortly after babies are born, they can demonstrate the ability to remember. Your memory is attached to the five senses: touch, smell, taste, sight, and hearing. You probably have vivid memories in each one of those categories. For sure you will never forget having your baby. Certain memories will be recalled about the sights and sounds of that special day. Pray for your son or daughter to grow in the Lord and to always remember Him first in all things.

Pray your little ones will press on, ever anticipating the goodness of God in every circumstance. Pray that they will not hold on to their former life before Christ, but will forget the past (Philippians 3:12–14).

Praise the Lord for His grace and mercy and for forgetting your child's sin (Hebrews 8:12).

Pray your little one will always remember what is noble, just, pure, lovely, and worthy of praise (Philippians 4:8).

Momma,

Do you regularly remember the faithfulness of God? Be intentional today about calling to mind the times He has healed you, provided for you, and loved you. Write down, remember, and revisit His grace in your life. List just five things He has promised you in Christ, and pretty soon, you will be full of praise. Thankfulness will take root in your heart, and you will see God in all things.

Journal those promises and meditate on them for the next week.

day 229 incomparable

Momma, this day's entry is focused on **you** again, dear one. Look down at your bump. Do you feel like a superwoman, growing another human inside of you? Your eyes are likely automatically drawn to another pregnant momma at the store. Before your pregnancy, you may not have even noticed another momma-to-be, but now you feel like you see them everywhere. Are you curious? Do you ask how far along she is? Maybe you tend to start the conversation, comparing bellies. Your heart may feel a common bond with her, or you may feel a little frumpy by comparison.

Resolve not to become ensnared by looking at other moms, other children, and other lives and wishing for what they have. God is too creative to squeeze you into His vision for another sister. Psalm 139 is a great place to start when confessing the truth of who you are as His child.

Momma,

Do you tend to be ensnared by looking through the lens of comparison? Your great-great-great-times-a-bunch-grandmother, Eve, from the garden of Eden taught you to look at the life you cannot have and strive to get it. But Jesus teaches you, sister, that your God is King. In fact, He is the King of Kings (Revelation 19:16). He is so unlimited in His beauty that He made all of humanity in His image. His supply is enough. If He wanted two of you (or two Eves), He would have made two. Eve took the bait of the enemy because her eyes caused her to stumble. She took her eyes off the Father and was led astray by what she wanted and what she saw. So what do you want?

Keep beholding God and become fixed on who He is for you (2 Corinthians 3:18). His purposes for you and for the kingdom cannot be compared to anyone else's. His plan is personal, one-sized, just for you, and unique to you, beloved. You are wonderfully made.

day 230 satisfied

While your little one is being knit together, your own body is changing as well. You may have noticed a slight leaking of colostrum, the onset of breast milk. If you haven't noticed this, you're perfectly fine. This first milk is full of antibodies and powerful nutrition for your infant. God is already equipping your body to be your little one's source of food once he or she is born. Eating is essential for life. You may have fasted for a period of time or skipped a meal or two to pray, but eventually your body will need food for survival. Spiritual food is no different. Jesus calls Himself the Bread of Life (John 6:35), and consuming Him daily is the only way to live a Spirit-filled life. Pray your child will hunger for the things of God and not be satisfied with the emptiness of the world.

Pray your son or daughter will live by every word that comes from the mouth of God (Matthew 4:4).

Thank God that He promises to satisfy your little ones as they hunger and thirst for righteousness (Matthew 5:6). Ask God to bless them with a deep, unquenchable thirst for the Spirit.

Bless your child today with a contagious spirit so others will become hungry and thirsty for Jesus as they experience Him through your child.

Momma,

Your first milk will transition to more mature milk days and weeks after birth. Praise God that His Word, the pure milk, is unchanging truth. The Bible has been the source of life for this dark world. It has been debated over the centuries but never destroyed. God's Word has remained a light, revealing the truth that cannot be hidden. Scripture is the very wisdom and revelation of God Himself. It reveals Jesus and the Holy Spirit and describes how we are to walk in Him. If you struggle hearing from God, then listen to Him through His Word (Romans 10:17).

day 231 known

Today your baby can discern your voice. Your son or daughter will show a preference for your unique sound over that of another female, like an aunt or sibling. Do you talk to your baby? You may read books or sing to him or her. For now your little one is literally always hearing the sounds you make. In the coming years, your voice will also be distinguishable from others. In a crowd, your call will be personal and known by your child. Pray that in the same way your voice can guide and direct your little ones, their spiritual ears will discern the voice of the Spirit.

Ask God to give your child ears to hear so that they will be able to understand the wisdom of the Spirit (Matthew 11:15).

Ask God to plant faith in the heart of your son or daughter as they hear the Word through relationship (Romans 10:17).

Pray your little one will be quick to hear and slow to speak (James 1:19-27).

Bless your child as a kingdom seeker who will always look and listen for how God speaks in any circumstance (Mark 4:24).

Momma,

What is the Lord speaking to you in this season? Is it a scripture, a word, a promise? If you say He's not revealing anything new to you, go back and revisit what He said last. He wants you to obey when He has given direction. He wants you to trust when He has spoken. He wants to settle in your heart the last promise He gave you. Ask the Holy Spirit for fresh oil in your heart to remember and receive what God has done.

List words, pictures, and scriptures that come to mind:

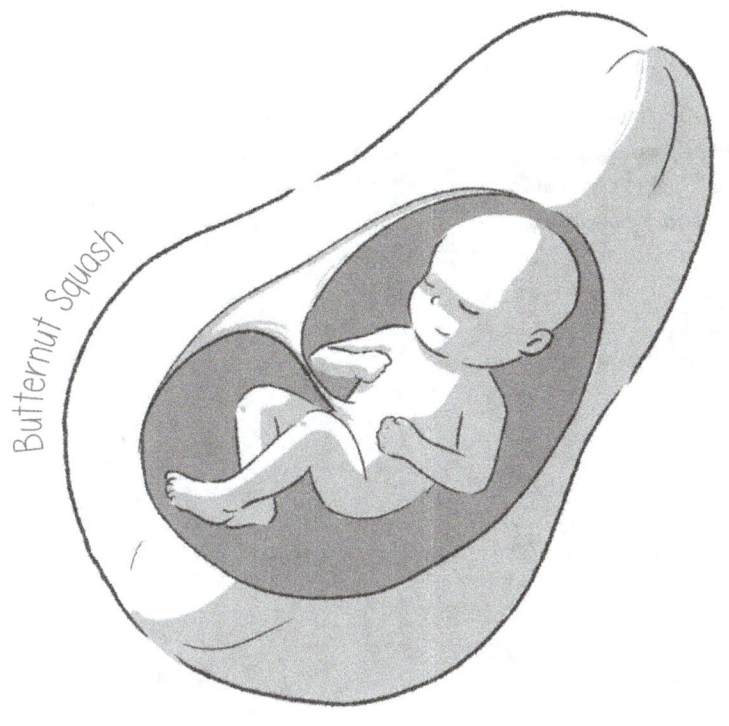

Butternut Squash

WEEK
thirty-four

day 232   behold

You're probably already guessing the color of your baby's eyes. It's one of the most anticipated moments after birth, looking over your baby's form and discovering different details like eye color. The eyes of most infants have a bluish hue, but within a month or so after birth, their permanent color will be set. Interestingly, babies can only see objects in black and white until the four-month mark. After that time a beautiful world comes alive to capture their young vision. Pray today for your son or daughter's spiritual vision, that they behold God in His glory and majesty.

Pray the Holy Spirit will give your child spiritual sight, enabling them to see how God sees: through the lens of love (Luke 4:18).

Thank God that He will open the eyes of your child so they can turn from darkness to light (Acts 26:18).

Ask that the eyes of your child's heart will be enlightened so they will know what their calling is (Ephesians 1:18).

Momma,

Is your spiritual vision single-hearted, 20/20, fixed on the Lord, despite the noise of the world? The first temptation Eve faced in the garden of Eden was targeted at her sight. The enemy knew then (and still knows now) that if he can delight your eyes with anything other than the beautiful One, he's got access to your heart. Meditate on Revelation 3:15–18 and let the Lord heal your sight. Jesus is altogether lovely and worthy of all our affection.

day 233 heaven's tongue

Your baby is not only listening to the sound of your voice, but will soon be able to interpret the language spoken. From very early on in their development, babies learn their parent's native tongue. English, Spanish, and other languages have distinct sounds and words. Language is the foundation of communication.

Babies learn the language you speak to them, even if you're bilingual. Beginning with simple words, your little ones will grow into speaking from a complex vocabulary by the time they reach adulthood. In the same way, as believers, you learn the language of heaven when you read God's Word. The Holy Spirit teaches you how to think and speak with the mind and wisdom of God. Pray today that your child will speak with the tongue of heaven which is full of love, wisdom, and grace.

Pray your son or daughter will pursue love and earnestly desire the spiritual gifts, especially the gift of prophecy (1 Corinthians 14:1). The gift of prophecy is simply proclaiming the Father's heart and will to upbuild, encourage, and comfort the body (1 Corinthians 14:3). Ask the Holy Spirit to teach your child how to think and speak like Jesus. He taught, prayed, healed, and proclaimed with authority given by God. His words were always rooted in love and truth. Pray Philippians 4:8 over your little one.

Momma,

What a miracle language is. You will see this very soon. As parents speak their baby's name over and over, day in and day out, the little ones will start responding by turning their heads. That's a sign your baby has learned its name. When God speaks to you, have you learned to recognize His voice? He can speak correction to your heart while completely engulfing you in love. He never speaks with condemnation or condescension, only grace, beloved.

day 234   filled

Babies have already begun to store vitamins and minerals, like iron, in their tiny bodies. God designed your body to thrive on nutrients, and He made provisions to store them for when there is a deficiency. Consider how God does this spiritually as well. When you need a promise for hope or help, God's Word comes to nourish your spirit. Pray today that God's Word will be hidden in the hearts of your son or daughter and that they will draw on it for life-giving nourishment.

Pray your child will not live by worldly wisdom or natural reasoning. Ask that the Word of Christ will dwell richly in their heart (Colossians 3:16).

Ask the Holy Spirit to teach your son or daughter to live by every word that God speaks and not merely look to social media, friends, or any other way that seems right (Luke 4:4).

Pray your child meditates day and night on the Word of God and hides it in their heart (Psalm 119:11).

Momma,

God's Word is truth. He calls it a sword of the Spirit (Ephesians 6:17). The Lord also calls it a light (Psalm 119:105). It can cut, heal, and reveal. How often are you letting the Holy Spirit use the Scriptures to expose, encourage, or renew your mind? You will live by natural reasoning and fleshly thoughts if you rarely engage with God's Word. Going to church and hearing a sermon is not a substitute for your own personal conversation with God. Today is a fresh opportunity to hear from Him, and it's as easy as asking, "Holy Spirit, where would you lead me in Your Word?"

day 235 patient

Babies born at this stage are smaller than full-term babies, but they can still thrive and grow with support outside the womb. Children experience growth and learn at different rates. Some are quick to grasp a concept, while others require additional nurturing. Your son or daughter is perfectly placed in God's timing and plan for their life. Pray for your child to get confidence from God as they see the growth of children around them.

Pray that your child will move beyond the elementary teachings about Christ and be taken forward to maturity (Hebrews 6:1).

Pray your child will crave pure spiritual milk so they grow up in their salvation (1 Peter 2:2-3).

Momma,

Be encouraged that you are perfectly placed in your transformation into Christ's likeness. God has given you the desire to obey Him and the power to do what pleases Him. Your transformation is His responsibility and great joy. Rest and trust that He is taking you forward into maturity and growing you up in your salvation.

day 236 precious

As your baby continues to develop, pray for his or her self-image to be redeemed and that they honor the Lord. You and your little one were both created in the image of God, designed to be just like Him in every way (Genesis 1:26). Just as God sees Himself holy and righteous, pray your son or daughter will walk in their identity in Christ, set apart from the world.

Declare Ephesians 1:3-5 over your little ones, that they are holy and blameless, adopted into the Father's family by faith.

Praise God that He will cause your child to walk as a child of light in this world (Ephesians 5:8).

Thank the Lord for His tender love, that He calls your child His very own (Isaiah 43:1).

Momma,

Your true identity is who God says you are. So who do you think you are, beloved? Do you walk in the reality that you are called by your Father a dearly loved child of God? Meditate today on Isaiah 43:4. He calls you precious.

day 237 named

As the day for your little one's arrival draws near, you may have already settled on a name, or perhaps you're still pondering the perfect fit and combination of names. With such a permanent decision, it would be wise to keep your spirit open to how the Lord would lead you. Names are special to Him, and you will find power and promise in the meaning of a name.

Praise God, who calls your child by name (Isaiah 43:1; 49:1).

Thank God for a particular aspect of His holy name that He will be for your child. He will be Father, wonderful Counselor, mighty God for them (Isaiah 9:6).

Create your own prayer, asking the Lord to reveal a name to you. Wait expectantly for His answer.

Momma,

The Lord calls Himself many names, like the Alpha and Omega, the beginning and the end. Some scholars record up to twenty-four names for God in the Bible! Examples include Jehovah Jireh, Jehovah Rapha, Jehovah Nissi, Jehovah Shalom, Jehovah Raah, Jehovah Tsidkenu, Jehovah Shammah, Abba Father, Adonai, Alpha and Omega, El Roi, Elohim, and El Elyon. Today He is your El Roi, "the God who sees" (Genesis 16:13). Have you ever looked up your own name to see what it means? You might find that it describes you exactly, which is no mistake. He sees you, beloved. You are surely the apple of His eye (Psalm 17:8).

day 238   heart

Congratulations. You've almost reached the last and final stretch of your pregnancy. As the countdown begins, you will probably notice you're nesting, or trying to organize and clean your home, in order to get ready for the baby. Spiritually, your heart is where Jesus longs to dwell. Pray for your heart today, Momma, that He will be welcomed into the deepest recesses and rooms of your soul.

Meditate on this scripture:

"I bow my knees before the Father, from whom every family in heaven and on earth is named, that according to the riches of his glory he may grant you to be strengthened with power through his Spirit in your inner being, so that Christ may dwell in your hearts through faith" (Ephesians 3:14-17).

Thank God for His desire to make your child's heart His permanent dwelling.

Momma,

Can't you see Jesus walking down the halls of your heart, looking for a place to rest? He loves being in your heart. He is at home there. He knows where everything is and is free to live there. Maybe there's a back room that has the door shut because it's messy and filled with clutter. Let Him come do the nesting for you. He will cleanse that place with His blood and fling the door open, broadening the space where He can dwell. Then He can roam from room to room while you say, "Go ahead. Make yourself at home."

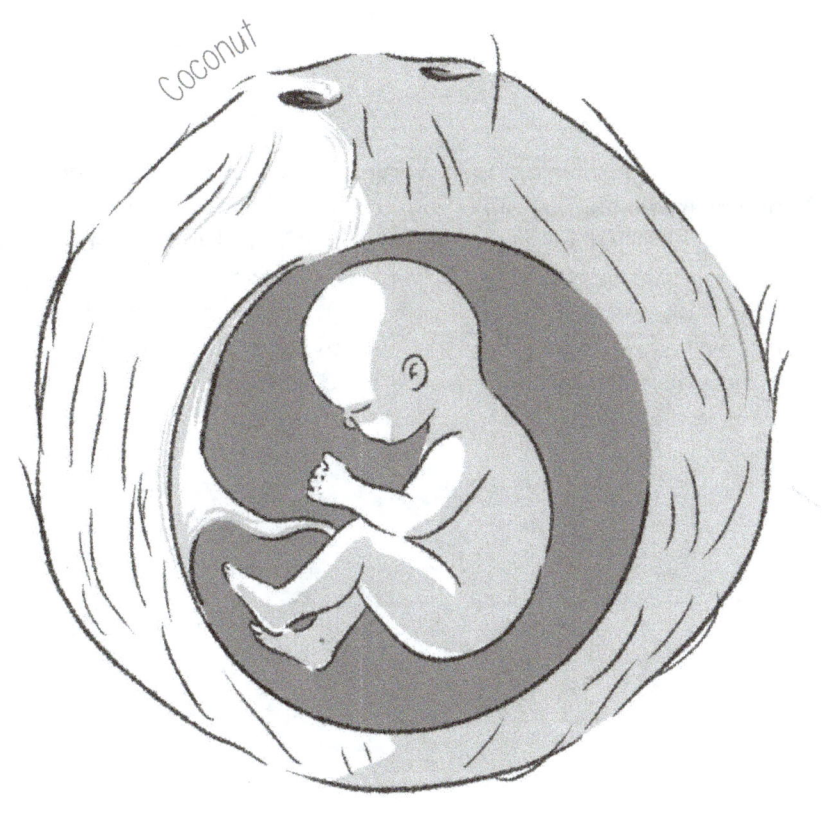

Coconut

WEEK

thirty-five

day 239 imitate

Your baby is developing a very complex brain, designed with the ability to mimic, or copy, your behaviors. You will likely erupt into squeals the first time your son or daughter waves bye-bye or blows kisses in response to yours. It will be the same when he or she imitates your faith. As you model forgiveness, grace, and love for Jesus, so, too, will your child. They won't know any other way. Pray for the atmosphere of your home to be filled with truth.

Proverbs 24:3-4 says, "By wisdom a house is built and by understanding it is established; by knowledge the rooms are filled with all precious and pleasant riches."

Pray that your home will be saturated with the wisdom of Christ, setting it apart as holy unto Him.

Pray that your little ones will receive the truth as you speak it over them.

Momma,

Maybe you've reflected on your childhood during this pregnancy. There may be some memories of things you want to imitate from your mother. And there are likely behaviors that you will not be carrying into your parenting. Rest assured that you have a perfect Father in heaven who will help you moment by moment and establish His goodness in your home.

day 240 — pain

As you prepare for your little one's birthday, maybe you've already weighed options for pain relief, if any, during birth. You've probably made a decision based on your health and preference. While you may be able to avoid physical pain during labor, emotional pain of the heart cannot always be avoided. However, it can always be healed by Jesus. Pray for your son or daughter's heart, that it would always be tender and receptive to God's healing touch and His Word.

Thank the Lord, who promises to be near to the brokenhearted and save the crushed in spirit (Psalm 34:18).

Praise God, who heals the brokenhearted and binds up their wounds (Psalm 147:3).

Pray for the peace of Jesus to surround the heart of your son or daughter. He promised to give them His peace, not the peace of this world (John 14:27).

Momma,

As you pray for your child, is there one thing you really, really hope would never touch them? Did an old wound or fear come to mind? Oftentimes it's not an event that comes to your heart, but an emotion that touches your soul, leaving you with a sense of gloom. Invite Jehovah Rapha to heal the depths of your heart and restore you to peace. His perfect love will cast out every fear (1 John 4:18).

day 247   spirit

Your baby's kidneys have matured. What a feat for such a little human. Kidneys are the body's major organ for excreting waste and producing hormones. These important bean-shaped organs help your body regulate fluid levels. While God has equipped our bodies with regulators, He has also given us the Holy Spirit to be our teacher, who helps us to discern between good and evil.

Praise the Lord, who knows the mind of the Spirit and who intercedes on behalf of your child (Romans 8:27).

Thank God, who sent His Spirit, the Helper, who convicts the world concerning sin and righteousness and judgment (John 16:7-11). Thank Him for the way He will teach and help your child walk in the Lord.

Pray that, as your child matures, they will test the spirits to see whether they are from God (1 John 4:1). God will grant them the wisdom needed to distinguish between truth and falsehood (James 1:5).

Momma,

Wisdom is defined as having God's thoughts and ways about all things in life. The Lord promises to give wisdom to all who ask for it (James 1:5). Ask Him for it, and He will provide it exceedingly abundantly. You can gather your thoughts, but the Lord will always give you the right answer (Proverbs 16:1). What do you need wisdom for today?

day 242 bridal love

The very core of a baby's body, the heart, is monitored by your practitioner. Once born, during the early days of sleep, a baby's heart rate remains constant. As you speak and interact with your baby, their heart rate actually slows down because they are attentive to your voice. Pray that your child's spiritual heart will respond to the love and voice of God in a similar way, recognizing His voice as one to be attentive to.

Pray that your son or daughter will seek God's face with their whole heart (Psalm 27:8).

Ask God to give your child bridal love like that found in Song of Solomon. The bride says to her beloved, "Draw me after you" (Song of Solomon 1:4).

Pray that your child will "not be anxious about tomorrow, for tomorrow will be anxious for itself" and that they will know that "all these things will be added to [them]" because their "heavenly Father knows that [they] need them all" (Matthew 6:33-34).

Momma,

As you pray for your child's heart to be responsive to the love of Christ, have you considered the ways He has pursued you today? Read the passionate exchanges between a bride and her lover in Song of Solomon today. You are that bride. He longs for all of your affection, beloved. Don't hold back. Pour it out on Him as Mary of Bethany did, with unbridled emotion and expectation.

day 243 sovereign

You may be discussing with your practitioner the details of delivery, depending on any risk factors you may be experiencing. For example, if you're having high blood pressure, you're being monitored more closely, and your baby may require a Cesarean birth. Timing is important. And spiritually, God is sovereign, aligning all things in your child's life in His perfect timing, right down to the birth.

Praise the Lord for His love over you and your baby. He alone knows all things and has every circumstance subjected to His lordship (Hebrews 2:8).

Thank Him for His impeccable timing. He has ordered every footstep of your life and makes your way perfect (Psalm 18).

Thank Him that when you are afraid, you can put your trust in Him (Psalm 56:3)

Mediate on these verses: "The LORD is my light and my salvation; whom shall I fear? The LORD is the stronghold of my life; of whom shall I be afraid?" (Psalm 27:1).

"Peace I leave with you; my peace I give you. Not as the world gives do I give to you. Let not your hearts be troubled, neither let them be afraid" (John 14:27).

Momma,

May you be comforted by the perfect care of your Father. He says to you, "Daughter, there is no need to fear and control what you can see, and especially those things you cannot see." He is proving Himself to you daily and training you to trust Him. In this place, there is peace and rest.

day 244 *glory to glory*

In these last few weeks, maybe you've been studying the ultrasound pictures you've been given. The 3-D images are incredibly clear. Do you already see similarities to your facial features? Does he have your nose? Does she have your mouth? God's design of your little one is absolutely perfect. He loves making you in His image. As He changes you from glory to glory (2 Corinthians 3:18), He reveals the beauty of His Son (Romans 8:29).

Praise God that He promises to work all things together for the good of those who love Him and walk according to His purpose, ever making you into the image of Jesus (Romans 8:28-29).

Thank Him for the multiplication of His beautiful image on the earth through the body of Christ.

Ask that your little one be conformed to the image of God (Romans 12:2).

Momma,

Think of your current circumstances. Ask God, "How are you using this to reveal Christ to me?" And follow up with, "What fruit are you producing in me because of this situation?" Don't curse your troubles; cast all your cares on Him, because He cares for you (1 Peter 5:7, 1 Peter 1:6-7).

day 245 like no other

You may be getting a glimpse into your baby's personality. He or she may love to nuzzle up on one side, preferring a spot under your ribs. While that can be uncomfortable, you will be holding your son or daughter very soon. You will get to discover the creativity of God. He has gifted your child with their own unique talents, gifts, and preferences. Part of the fun of parenting is discovering who they are.

Today, immerse yourself in Psalm 139. Consider reading it in different translations. It will bring a beautiful fullness to the Word. Several Bible apps make it easy to compare versions.

Thank God that all creation glorifies Him. He has one purpose for everything He makes: to bring Him glory. Your child, too, will showcase His magnificence. Spend a few moments praising Him for something specific, something that causes you to respond, "Wow, Lord! You made _____!"

Momma,

Have you experienced the thought of how surreal pregnancy can be? How fascinating that God is forming another human being in your womb. Meditate on the miracle of it all. What have you learned about pregnancy that shows you the majesty and power of your creator?

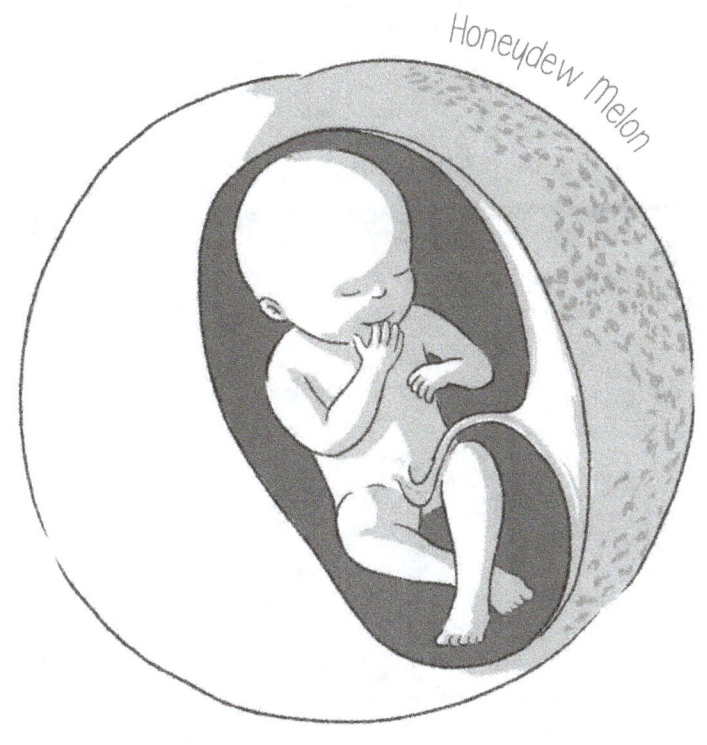

Honeydew Melon

WEEK

thirty-six

day 246   unique

While babies are inside the womb, they are in a mini classroom. Your baby is learning, even from the stimuli outside the womb like music, your voice, or even loud noises. Your child is a born learner. God designed children's minds to be inquisitive and ever curious. Even as your child matures, pray that God would daily nourish their childlike faith in unique and personal ways.

Pray that your child would grow in the example of Jesus, who increased in wisdom and stature and favor with God and man (Luke 2:52).

Thank God for the way He made your child think and learn. They may learn differently from the way their siblings learn, but this only highlights God's unique and personal design of your child. He has given your son or daughter the mind of Christ (1 Corinthians 2:16).

Momma,

Learning the Christ-life will last until you see Jesus face-to-face. You are learning even now as you pray for your baby's physical and spiritual development, but the greatest learning is in the Holy Spirit. He is the best teacher and loves to see you grow. In the kingdom classroom, what is He teaching you now? If you're not sure, ask Him. He will tutor you, supply extra practice, and encourage you in the process. You can't fail His tests, daughter, because His love promises to work all things together for your good and His glory.

day 247 faith-full

You already love your baby, and you haven't even met him or her yet. How awesome that God's design is to place such deep affection inside of you for someone you've yet to behold. Your love is truly an act of faith. Pray that your child comes to know the love of Jesus and that they will love Him even though they cannot see Him.

First Peter 1:8 says, "Though you have not seen him, you love him. Though you do not now see him, you believe in him and rejoice with joy that is inexpressible and filled with glory." Praise God for the portion of faith He has given your child to believe Him and His Word.

Declare that your son or daughter will "walk by faith, not by sight" (2 Corinthians 5:7) and that they will live as the righteous, by faith alone (Hebrews 10:38).

Momma,

Faith is the only way to live in God. He does miracles, moves mountains, and multiplies the minuscule by one method: faith. If you're depending more on the seen than the unseen, ask Him to help your unbelief (Mark 9:23-25). He loves to be asked. And He loves to answer.

day 248 adored

You already know how you feel about your baby, but have you considered how your child will view itself? How heartbreaking to think they could believe any lie that causes them to think they are less than the wonderful and beautiful handiwork of their loving Father. Pray that your son or daughter will see themself as completely approved and adored.

Praise God, who chose your child before the foundation of the world, that they should be holy and blameless before Him (Ephesians 1:4).

Believe God for the following reality: your child will love their neighbor the way they love themself (Matthew 22:39).

Insert your child's name as you read and pray Psalm 139 over your baby, for example: "Marie is fearfully and wonderfully made."

Momma,

Self-love seems contrary to Christ's call to die to ourselves. The two are not the same. The difference is the emphasis on self. Your Father wants you to see yourself the way He made you: perfectly and wonderfully. Death to yourself is letting the Lord purge any sin that mars His precious creation. Sin has no place in your life. Ask Him to give you fresh love for yourself.

Did you know that when your little ones are born, they will see the world as a colorless spectrum of black, white, and gray until they are about three months of age? Praise God for the beautiful and vivid world He gave us to explore, but nothing compares to the explosive colors in heaven. Pray your child will bring the kingdom of heaven to earth.

You may be familiar with the Lord's Prayer, but stop and ask the Holy Spirit to fill you as you read this over your child. It's found in Matthew 6:9-13.

Our Father in heaven,

Hallowed be Your name,

Your kingdom come in _____'s life,

Your will be done in _____'s life,

On earth as it is in heaven.

Give _____ this day her/his daily bread,

And forgive _____ his/her debts as _____ forgives his/her debtors.

And lead _____ not into temptation,

But deliver _____ from evil.

Momma,

Now pray this same verse over yourself.

day 250 living water

One of the best ways to combat swelling in the last weeks is to drink plenty of water. An increase in fluid will help flush excess sodium from your body, preventing swelling. God designed your body to depend on water, this amazing fluid, every day. Without it, life could not be sustained. In the same way, Jesus offers the living water of Himself to anyone who thirsts. Pray that God will stir up a holy thirst for the Lord at a young age in your child.

Pray that your child will believe in Jesus and that from their innermost being will flow rivers of living water (John 7:37–39).

Ask God to empower your son or daughter to abide in the fountain of living water (Jeremiah 17:13).

Thank God that your child will never thirst or desire another once they partake of Christ.

Momma,

Have you ever experienced the Holy Spirit like He is a river streaming through you? Jesus spoke of Himself as living water. He is not stale or stagnant but vibrant and bubbling over. Just like water is essential for physical life, Jesus presents Himself as essential for spiritual life and fulfillment. Once you consume Him, nothing else satisfies or refreshes you the same. He comes erupting back up as a wellspring from within you every time you call on Him. You cannot contain Him. Drink, daughter, and be satisfied.

day 251 hearing

Your little one's ability to hear has fully developed. It can even discern in what direction a sound is being made. It's true. At birth, you may immediately see the miracle of your baby turning its head in the direction of your voice. Jesus's voice is distinct, and He speaks via His Spirit. Pray that your child will have keen spiritual hearing.

Thank God that He hears your child's cries for help (2 Samuel 22:7, Psalm 3:4, Isaiah 65:24).

Praise Him that He created your little one in His image. Pray your son or daughter will hear the Word of God, understand it, and bear fruit (Matthew 13:23).

Momma,

Hearing is a gift, but those who cannot hear are often good at lip reading. If you don't sense the Lord speaking, trust His silence and become an expert at reading His heart. If you've been anxious about hearing Him, the key is to keep abiding in him anyway (John 15:5). His voice might be playful, firm, excited, or a whisper. Press into the Lord's heart so you can hear how He is speaking to you. He speaks in so many ways—a breeze on your face on a hot day, the exact Bible verse you needed to read, a call from a caring friend, or as an answer to prayer.

day 252 discern

Once your baby arrives, it will have more face-to-face interaction with you than with any other human. They love gazing at your face, lingering longer with each passing month of maturity. They also respond to objects of light over other stimuli. From the beginning, God created light as a reflection of His glory. He is light, and in Him there is no darkness (1 John 1:5). Pray that as your child grows, God will shine His light in their heart.

Ask Jesus to grant the light of His life to your child (John 8:12).

Praise God that His light shines in the darkness, and the darkness will not overcome it (John 1:5). No matter where your child should go, the light of Jesus can shine there, bringing salvation. Ask God to fill your child with confidence that they cannot be overcome by the kingdom of darkness.

Pray that your son or daughter will let their light shine so others may see their good deeds and bring glory to their Father in heaven (Matthew 5:16).

Thank God that He will make your child like a city on a hill. Ask that your son or daughter will never attempt to hide their light, but rather boldly let them shine (Matthew 5:14).

Momma,

You may know what it's like to stumble in a dark room when the power goes out. You immediately start lighting candles or looking for your phone flashlight. God promises that His Word will be a light to guide you (Psalm 119:105). The Scriptures reveal God's design for your life, and it also reveals who God is for you in every circumstance. What word do you need to shed light, or truth, on in your life right now?

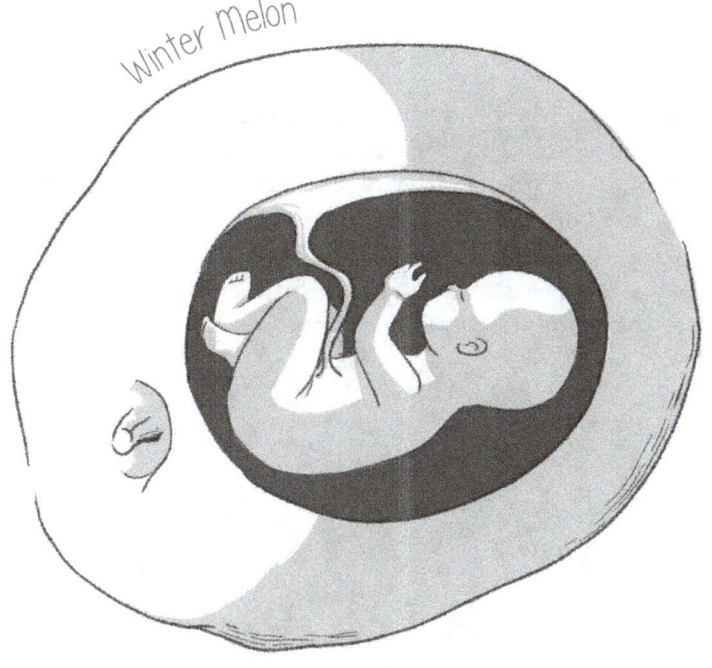

Winter Melon

WEEK

thirty-seven

day 253 — see

Your baby will be born with the ability to see, albeit only in black and white for the first few months. Over time, the eye will mature and begin seeing color. The perception of color makes life much more interesting. If we only saw in black and white, we would miss the beauty of God's creation. In the same way, pray that your son or daughter will see through eyes of love toward all colors of humanity. God's heavenly design was to create races from every color spectrum, and they are all beautiful because each one reflects Him.

Praise God that there is neither Jew nor Greek, slave nor free, male nor female, for we are all one in Christ Jesus (Galatians 3:28). Pray that your children will know their identities in Jesus and will treat others according to their identity in Him.

Ask God to give your son or daughter love for other races that flows from His own heart so your child will see others as being created in the image of God (Genesis 1:27).

Rejoice that your child will be among those saved from every tribe, people, and language. Ask the Father to grant your little one a heart that shows no partiality (Revelation 5:9-10).

Momma,

It is no secret that the world is a deeply divided place. But God has given you a peek into the heavenly realms with scenes from the book of Revelation, where we see people who don't look like us or speak like us all gathered in the same place, worshiping their Father. Can you imagine the color and beauty? May He grant you new vision to see not the outward differences of others, creating boundaries, but rather perceiving the beauty of the heart. He is just preparing you for heaven.

Today, you can settle your heart around the birth. Within just a few weeks, you will meet the one you've been praying for. You may have imagined how your birth will take place and may have even created a birth plan. The pinnacle of your journey is near. Everything you've endured while carrying a child in your womb will be worth it when you see that precious face for the first time.

Pray this: Father, thank You for covering every detail of my delivery. You know the day, time, and hour You will usher this little soul into the world. I praise You now for the peace, strength, and grace You will supply as I give birth. You are the great deliverer, ready to see Your plans fulfilled on earth as they are in heaven (Ephesians 3:20).

Bless the doctors, nurses, hospital staff, and all who will help in your delivery. Thank the Lord for His abundant provision for your recovery and postdelivery.

Thank Him that joy will be the atmosphere of your birth and that His smile will overshadow your child's arrival. Be filled with expectation for Your goodness.

Momma,

You're also pregnant with dreams He has placed in you. What are they? Maybe becoming a mother is fulfilling part of that dream. Sit in His presence. Worship Him in a song or a reading. Ask Him to open the imagination of your heart to see what He longs to give you. What does He say? Your prayer and expectation stir your faith in God. When your child comes to you one day, asking for a gift with full assurance that you will give it, a joyful trust is built. Even if you should have to deny a gift, they will know your deep love for them. Let faith fill your heart for how God is purifying your desires. He is the best gift and loves to be given.

day 255   wait

Your baby is in the thirty-fifth week of gestation. Every organ is in place and functioning; it's best for him or her to stay snuggled in your womb until the due date, but if your baby were to be born prematurely, their likeliness of thriving is high. Praise God for advances in medicine that help preemies develop normally. Spiritually, just as your little one is waiting to be born, pray that they will wait on the Lord as they grow. He promises that your child's strength will be renewed in Him as they wait (Isaiah 40:31).

Praise God for the way He waits to be gracious to your child (Isaiah 30:18).

Pray that your son or daughter will be still and know the Lord (Psalm 46:10). Thank the Father for the way He will teach your child to wait and not go ahead of Him.

God promises His goodness to your child as they wait on Him (Lamentations 3:25). Praise Him for the way He will reveal His goodness in the waiting.

Pray that your little one's heart is strengthened with courage as he or she waits on the Lord (Psalm 27:14).

Momma,

You wait all the time: at the doctor's office, in grocery lines, and while sitting in traffic. How you spend your time waiting is important. Psalm 33:20-21 says, "Our soul waits for the LORD; he is our help and our shield. For our heart is glad in him, because we trust in his holy name." As you wait, the Lord often draws you to deeper worship and intimacy with Him so He can produce His joy in you. He is not letting you move one step until His promise has been established in your heart. So take heart, sister. He is waiting to give you the gift of Himself.

day 256   help!

Your little one is likely making different faces at you right now while you're dreaming of who he or she favors. Do they have Mom's nose? Dad's eyes? Their face reveals so much, especially genetic traits and emotions. Children have a simple way to let you know they're not happy: crying. God designed your baby with the ability to cry as a sign that something needs to be fixed. Babies' cries are the only way they know to ask for help. As your child grows, they mature, and they will be able to articulate what is wrong. The Father promises to be near to your child as they ask for help.

Thank God that He is an ever-present help for your child in times of trouble (Psalm 46:1).

Praise Jesus, who is able to sympathize with the weaknesses of your son or daughter. Pray that they will come boldly to the throne of grace, obtaining mercy and finding grace in time of need (Hebrews 4:15–16).

Rejoice when the Lord helps your child, and teach them to thank God for His unfailing love in every trial (Psalm 63:3).

Momma,

Your heavenly Father is able. Period. When you experience trials and just want to cry to Him for help, He is closer than your very breath. Hold to the promise that He works everything for your good as you love Him (Romans 8:28). Only God can bring good from bad, and He loves who He is making you in the process. Not one thing is wasted, no tear nor wordless cry from the heart. He longs to show you His love and draw you into His presence, casting His safe shadow on every trial. When you have Him in the midst of the fire, you can thank Him for purifying your heart. You will receive more of Him and His love, and that pain will serve its beautiful purpose.

day 257   grace

What a gift you're carrying. You've been praying daily for the body, soul, and spirit of your son or daughter. You can envision beautiful moments together for their future. You will be an example of God's love to your child. You will also have days when you make mistakes in the training of your little one. You may respond in frustration, but God is abundantly willing to offer you grace and forgiveness. Pray that as your child matures, the Lord will grant them a heart full of grace and mercy as you parent them.

Praise God that there is no condemnation in Christ for either you or your child (Romans 8:1).

Pray that your son or daughter will be merciful, just as their Father is merciful (Luke 6:36).

Ask God that He would grant your child the ability to bear with others and forgive them, as He forgives (Colossians 3:13).

Thank God for His love, which covers a multitude of sins (1 Peter 4:8).

Pray 1 Corinthians 13:4-8, inserting God's name in each attribute of love: "God is love. God is patient."

Momma,

As you learn to parent your little one, you will have greater understanding of the Father's perfect love of you. You will be filled with hope because His love is not like any earthly love. Spend time praising Him for the way He will show you love in the smallest of ways, highlighting the deeply personal way He cares for His children. The Holy Spirit will perfect your ability to receive the Father's love. In what area of your heart do you most need His love to reign?

day 258 learn

Your baby is continuing to grow, filling up your tummy. Your bundle of joy is almost here, and you are likely anticipating being able to touch your own toes again. These next weeks may seem slow in coming, but in the grand view, your little one will be school age in just a few short years. Imagine them learning their numbers and how to read in about sixty months' time!

Praise God that He promises to instruct and teach your child in the way they should go, counseling them with His loving eye (Psalm 32:8).

Pray that the Word of Christ will dwell richly in your child and that they will be able to teach and admonish others with all wisdom (Colossians 3:16).

Ask that your child will take on the yoke of Jesus and learn from His humility and gentleness (Matthew 11:29-30).

Pray that your little one will honor those who teach them, including parents, grandparents, teachers, and church leadership (Romans 13:1-10).

Momma,

You are about to go to school, enrolling in Parenting 101 (or 201). Whether this is your first baby or fifth, you will always be learning what kind of loving parent God is. He has never made one mistake in parenting, and you are made in His image. He will teach you to become just like Him. The Holy Spirit promises to teach you all things and remind you of everything Jesus has spoken (John 14:26). Your Daddy whispers, "Come sit in My lap," when you just need to be comforted. After all, He is the very author of the mother's heart. "As one whom his mother comforts, so I will comfort you" (Isaiah 66:13).

day 259 dependent

Today, as your baby is growing, take time to think about the creativity of God. His design of human life is both profound and majestic. You've been praying for months over these tiny details: eyelids, fingertips, and toes. Have you considered that the same God might tell you to become childlike in your faith? Jesus said unless you change and become like a little child, you will never enter the kingdom of heaven (Matthew 18:2-4). Why is that? He knows that children are completely dependent on their parents and helpless apart from them. Pray that you will take the lowly position of a child as you raise this little one.

Thank Jesus for His heart toward your child and that He desires always that they come to Him (Matthew 19:14).

Ask the Father to give you wisdom as you train your son or daughter, knowing that when they are older, they will not depart from your godly instruction (Proverbs 22:6).

Think of who Jesus calls the greatest in the kingdom—children (Matthew 18:1-14). Thank Him for His esteem of your child's faith.

Momma,

You, too, are a kid! You're the King's daughter. He loves doing life with you and giving you life. His greatest delight is fulfilling His promises to you. What part of your heart is being purified in this season? That's the very place He will make you an overcomer. Have you allowed Him in? His call is for you to become child**like**, not child**ish**. How freeing to crawl up on His lap, that safest of places, and tell Him the desires of your heart, pour out your secret dreams, and reveal your hurts. Lean into His chest. Feel His strength engulfing you. Your every care is swallowed up in His love. Oh, the security of your Daddy's heart.

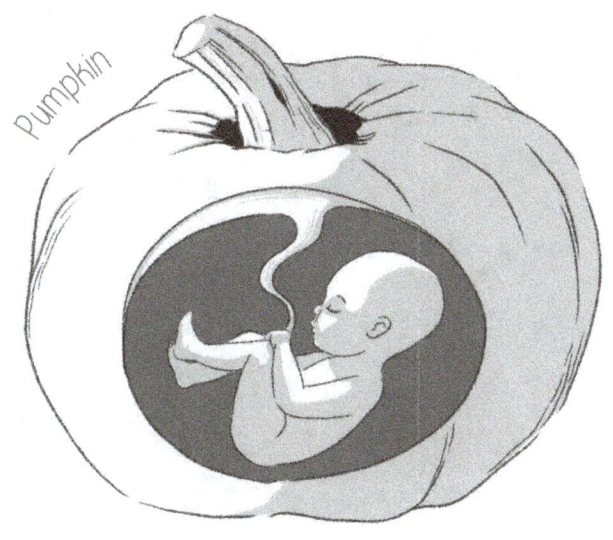

Pumpkin

WEEK

thirty-eight

day 260   shine

Your child's life has been conceived in the heart of God, his or her every day numbered already (Psalm 139:16). God is knitting your son or daughter together in His image. Can you fathom the depth of His love for your little one? Every moment, every struggle, every victory, every breath already has provision attached to it. The world is lost and dark. Your child has been called to be a light, shining the good news and proclaiming hope to desperate souls.

Pray that your son or daughter will be bold in their love for God and others. Ask that the Father fill your child with radical love that manifests in radical mercy, grace, and truth—love they have received from the Father (1 Corinthians 16:14).

God is love, and He says whoever lives in love, lives in Him. Pray that they will be perfected in love (1 John 4:16-18) and that they would do good to their enemies without expecting to get anything back. Pray your child will be kind to the ungrateful and wicked (Luke 6:35).

Pray that love and faithfulness will never leave your child but be bound around their neck and written on the tablet of their heart. Pray your child will win favor and a good name in the sight of God and others (Proverbs 3:3-4).

Momma,

You cannot give away a thousand dollars if you don't have that amount of money. Sure, you can write a check for that amount, but there's no truth in the check. In the same way, you may offer the appearance of kindness or forgiveness to others with no real power. In fact, it may only empower self-righteousness. Genuineness, power, and wisdom are found in true giving. You know that you're only able to give what you've personally received. The Holy Spirit wants to make you both a great receiver and a great giver. Hallelujah.

day 267 overcome

Your little one already has the ability to sweat. Typically, the body will sweat as a cooling mechanism when it gets too hot. How awesome is the Father's design? In the same way, God gives your child the fruit of the Spirit as a way to combat the world and sin. Where there's fear, He gives love. Peace for anxiety. Self-control in place of chaos. In the face of a harsh world, He comes to give your son or daughter the fruit of gentleness. He is so good at giving these gifts to His children.

Praise God for the empowerment of the Holy Spirit in your son or daughter so they will walk in wisdom from above, which is pure, peace-loving, considerate, submissive, full of mercy and good fruit, impartial, and sincere (James 3:17). These virtues are the water a weary world so desperately thirsts for. Imagine your child walking in these, taking plunder from the enemy as God leads them in one victory after another.

Ask the Spirit to give you true discernment and insight in how to pray for your son or daughter in each season. For example, if they battle against fear, pray that God will supply abundant love that casts out fear (1 John 4:18).

Momma,

It is for freedom that Christ makes you free (Galatians 5:1). You were called and empowered to walk in absolute and total freedom. This means that you are not bound to anything or anyone but Christ. Other things like jobs and relationships lose their power to affect you. They lose their control. And the only things able to control you are Christ and His love (2 Corinthians 5:14–15). Praise God that with Him you overcome.

day 262 discipline

Your little one is almost here. Take heart, Momma; God hears your prayers as each one goes up before Him like sweet-smelling incense (Psalm 141:2). It is difficult to imagine the day when you will have to discipline your little one. How precious are those early years when they learn what to do and how to obey you. God says that discipline is necessary. In fact, it shows that you are His child when He disciplines you, even though it is sorrowful to Him (Hebrews 12:5-11). The beautiful news is that the discipline produces righteousness and peace. Praise God.

Pray that your child will obey your instructions willingly and without complaint (Ephesians 6:1). Ask that the Father will enable you to discipline as He disciplines, in love and with compassion.

Praise God for His wisdom as He disciplines you. He alone sanctifies you as you submit to Him. Thank Him for the good He is producing in you (Hebrews 12:10-11).

Momma,

The D-word. Discipline. It often carries a heaviness that can leave us wanting to think about other aspects of our walk with the Lord. Maybe you're thinking of discipline as punishment. The two are not the same. The Father never punishes you. Never. He cannot. He already punished His Son for you, as you. It's done. You will never pay for the things you do, are, say, or think. You will, as His daughter, be disciplined. Think of it as His training. It's the Father's way of teaching you to be as He is: perfect and complete, lacking nothing (James 1:4). In every season, He is training you to listen, abide, obey. In the area where you lack faith for obedience, He says, "C'mon, let's do it this way." The only thing really painful is the awareness of how much self remains alive in you. Let Him have His perfect way. A more peaceful and righteous you is around the corner.

day 263 distinct

Your little one is distinct in his or her gender. Think of all the differences between boys and girls besides anatomy. God purposed distinctions between male and female, and both work together for His glory on earth (Genesis 1:27). Pray that your son or daughter will be secure in the gender in which He created them and respect the opposite sex as God's creation.

Pray that the Father's heart will be manifested in your child so they see value in every human life, whether male or female (Galatians 3:27-28).

Ask that your child will walk humbly and not strive for control in any relationship.

Praise God for the beautiful purposes He longs to fulfill through your son or daughter, knowing that their gender was not random but purposed (Ephesians 2:10).

Pray that your child will walk with a single purpose and find their only true identity in being a child of God.

Ask the Lord to grant your child a heart to love and forgive those of the opposite sex if there be any offense from them (Proverbs 19:11).

Momma,

Those little baby kicks are reminders that you're chosen by God to carry this child in your body. Your belly is the first home your baby will know. Your husband cannot fully know the pregnancy and birth experience. And while many guys are thankful for that (!), you can see God's majesty from a totally different perspective—from the inside out. Praise your Father who, in His grace, allowed you to have this time to see His glory growing daily in you.

day 264 position

Your baby will change position if he or she has not already. They will shift or drop lower in your abdomen in preparation for birth. You are three and a half weeks away from your due date. This change in position will prove a delight since your breathing becomes noticeably easier. Similarly, God will often shift your child from one season to another in order to accomplish His will in their life. Pray for grace as His Spirit leads your child and that they will see God's transforming power in all circumstances.

Pray for your son or daughter to be transformed by the renewing of their mind and for them not conform to the thought pattern of the world (Romans 12:2).

Thank Jesus that He has handpicked every circumstance in your child's life for one purpose: intimacy. Praise Him that as your child draws near to God, He will draw near to your child (James 4:8).

Pray that your son or daughter will bless the Lord at all times (Psalm 34:1).

Ask God to grant your son or daughter a gracious spirit in times of trial, counting it all joy, knowing that the testing of their faith produces steadfastness (James 1:2-3).

Momma,

Seeing God in all things will free you to cooperate with the Spirit. Looking at a situation in the natural may cause you to grumble that you will be happy when it is over, but you can be happy now. God never wants to delay your joy. He is always trying to produce His fruit in you. It obviously does not mean your circumstances will always be pleasant, but He wants you to shine regardless. Never forget that no matter how dark it becomes, you, dear, are the light of the world (Matthew 5:14).

day 265 receive

In just a few short weeks, that little one you've seen on ultrasound pictures will be in your arms. How priceless that moment will be. Once your baby arrives, he or she will become the biggest receiver from you. Babies receive everything from you: love, food, attention. Everything they need to live will come from you. In the same way, spiritually, pray that your child will be a receiver. All that your son or daughter needs for the heart and soul will be provided through the Father.

Pray that your child will live in complete dependence on the Father, just as Jesus did (John 1:10; 15:5).

Ask that your son or daughter live out of the overflow of intimacy with the Lord and not strive to have an outward form of religion (Matthew 23:27).

Thank God, who promises that whatever your child asks for in prayer, if they believe they will receive it, will be given (Mark 11:24).

Pray that your child's heart will be open to receive from the Spirit, not limiting Him in any way.

Momma,

If you're a natural giver, receiving may be something the Lord wants to teach you. Sometimes your giving can actually be bondage because it flows from pride or the need to be needed. A river cannot flow unless it has a source of water. Spiritually, true giving only comes from true receiving. Jesus longs to pour into you His heart, His love, His mercy, His forgiveness. The natural byproduct of this pouring will be an overflow to those around you. It won't be forced or contrived. Simply, you will give as you receive. Hold your hands up as an outward sign to the Lord that you want more of Him today.

day 266 character

You are now almost thirty-seven weeks pregnant, and with that comes a very full womb. Your baby is snuggling close to your ribs. Perhaps you're being kicked by an elbow or foot. You may have even created a nickname for your baby that's related to its movement. In fact, you may be surprised that its tiny personality in the womb may be preparation for outside the womb. God gives children distinct personalities. He will bring glory to Himself through the unique way He has made yours. Being reserved, outgoing, comical, or serious can manifest and showcase the beautiful character of the Father.

Praise God, who created your little one in His very own image (Genesis 1:27) with emotions and a distinct personality graciously given by Him.

Thank the Father that His ultimate goal is to have hope springing up in your child.

Ask that your child will walk in loving discernment and be able to know good company from bad (1 Corinthians 15:33).

Pray that your child will bear with the weaknesses of others and not hold grudges. Ask God to fill their hearts with grace and mercy and for them to always treat others the way they want to be treated (Matthew 7:12).

Momma,

You're watching that bump and already discovering little clues about your baby's personality. How fun to watch her or him grow and to see that God-design unfold before your eyes. This is the Father's heart for you, beloved. He adores watching you become more and more like His Son. Everything you're currently going through is for the sole purpose of transforming you into the beautiful image of Jesus.

Watermelon

WEEK

thirty-nine

day 267   security

Your baby's birthday is almost here. The second you hear that tiny cry, you will be smitten. But that cry will be more significant than just a call to announce "Hey, world. I'm here." Your little one wants the familiar warmth and dimness of your tummy. Your precious baby is crying for you. One day, he or she may be comforted by a blankie or a pacifier, so enjoy the early moments when only your arms will do. Pray that your growing child will find all their security and comfort in the Father.

Praise God for His awesome love for your child. Absolutely nothing they can do will ever be able to separate them from God's perfect, sustaining love (Romans 8:35-39). What security!

Ask that your child would know the provision of God's presence in every circumstance in life (Psalm 23:1). Thank Him that He longs to manifest His comfort to your son or daughter in all seasons.

Pray for perfect love to cast out every fear your child might experience (1 John 4:18). Ask that He would turn your child's heart to Him for nothing more than intimacy with the Father.

Momma,

Just like your little one, you may experience a season that is unfamiliar and you've never walked this particular path before. Take heart. You have the best Parent who longs to teach you. He is the Lord of patience, the Lord of grace, and the Lord of gentleness. He will show you His goodness in the unfamiliar. When you cry for His presence, He will hold you tight, calming every fear. "I have calmed and quieted my soul like a weaned child with its mother; like a weaned child is my soul within me" (Psalm 131:2).

day 268 childlike

Your full-term baby is due soon. In fact, you may get to celebrate his or her birthday any day. You will assume a brand-new identity: Momma. It can be both exciting and a little daunting. What will my baby be like? How will I adjust after birth? And while you cannot answer those questions yet, one truth will carry you through motherhood: you won't know it all. Mothering requires constant learning and adapting. Having a teachable, childlike dependence on the Spirit will be key to walking in peace and rest. Pray the Father will give you humility as you raise this precious little one.

Praise God for the way He calls you to be simple and childlike in your faith. You will not see His kingdom in your own wisdom (Matthew 18:3).

Pray that the Father will open your eyes to His humility and cause you to repent of pride and self-sufficiency (1 Peter 5:6-7).

Thank God for His unlimited wisdom. Ask Him for wisdom in all circumstances; He promises to give it (James 1:5).

Momma,

You learn by asking lots of questions. Your Daddy in heaven delights in all your questions. He longs for you to come to Him. He is childlike in His ways, even playful. If you've never experienced this beautiful aspect of His character, seek Him by becoming simple in your thoughts. You will miss the wonder of seeing the way He sees if you're trying to have understanding apart from Him. His love is profound and yet so incredibly simple to receive. Confess to Jesus today: I need more of Your simplicity in my way of seeing.

day 269 *perfect timing*

Your hormones are working in perfect harmony as your body prepares for labor. Your level of estrogen has increased so that your cervix can be prepared to give birth to your little one. This process of softening your cervix happens near your baby's due date. God is so wonderfully perfect in His design, causing your body to get ready. At just the perfect moment, your muscles will begin to contract, hormones will be released, and soon after, you will meet your precious child. He already knows your baby's birthday, down to the second. Praise God for His perfect timing.

Praise God that He makes all things beautiful in their time (Ecclesiastes 3:11). He has been forming your little one for many months in your womb, delighting over each detail.

Pray that your child will number their days and gain a heart of love. Pray that your child will walk in wisdom at a young age (Psalm 90:12).

Thank God that His timing is not human or earthly. He is not slow in keeping His promises to you or your child (2 Peter 3:8-9). All time is His, and He is neither early nor late. Meditate on this today.

Momma,

Have you found comfort in God's perfect timing? Sometimes you may feel tempted to be impatient for an answer to prayer, but impatience is not from faith. God says love is patient. When you trust His perfect love, you will trust His timing is perfect. "Wait for the LORD; be strong, and let your heart take courage; wait for the LORD!" (Psalm 27:14).

day 270 prepared

Have you prepared for the birth of your little one? If you are choosing a hospital birth, now is the time to pack your bags with all the necessities. Some items to include are socks, comfy pajamas, toiletries, a nursing bra, and things for your newborn such as diapers, wipes, a swaddling blanket, and soft clothes to wear home. Be mindful of the season and pack accordingly. You may even feel up to gathering items for a nurse's blessing basket full of pens, gum, mints, and sticky notes. God is a planning God. He says He knows the plans He has for you (Jeremiah 29:11). He is carefully orchestrating all the details of your baby's birthday.

Ask God to help you commit all your ways to Him as He establishes your plans (Proverbs 16:3).

Thank Him that His ways are perfect. Pray that He will show you the way you should go as you trust Him (Psalm 143:8).

Today, dress or prepare your spirit with the full armor of God, dressing your spirit in truth, holding up a shield of faith, praying "at all times in the Spirit, with all prayer and supplication" (Ephesians 6:10-20).

Momma,

You have everything you need in Jesus. The greatest weapon is your faith, which is actually your biggest battle. Fighting the "good fight of the faith" (1 Timothy 6:12), as Paul said, will be the contention in every circumstance. Praise God today that He has already overcome as the Victor, ensuring you have won every trial you face. You're **more** than a conqueror!

day 271   peace

Your little one is another day closer to meeting Momma. You may be having signs of false labor, or Braxton-Hicks contractions. These tight squeezes around your belly are preparing your body for your real and active labor. While you may wonder at this point in pregnancy if the contractions you're feeling are real, your healthcare provider can help determine whether they are real or false. The Holy Spirit desires to give you peace in these last long days of pregnancy. Your sleeping, your eating, and even your sitting has possibly become more uncomfortable. Ask the Spirit to give you endurance and peace as you wait. You're close, Momma.

Thank God for His grace to give you joy as you wait on Him (James 1:2-3). The testing of your faith produces perseverance. Hallelujah.

Pray that your child will be strengthened with all power according to His glorious might so that they will have endurance and patience in every circumstance (Colossians 1:11).

Ask that your little one will grow to be joyful in hope, patient in affliction, and faithful in prayer (Romans 12:12).

Momma,

Read the last prayer prompt again. Did you spy that word "joyful"? As you wait, your hope is to be joyful. In Adam, you learned to be fretful and anxious as you wait, but in Jesus, your portion is peace and joy because these are beautiful fruits of His Spirit. These last few days of pregnancy are not just forming a baby; they can also fashion evidence of Jesus's joy in you. He said He wants His joy to be made full in you. Ask Him to produce this deep within you today.

Your life is about to change forever. In a few days, you will welcome another soul into this world. Look around. What is the current state of God's goodness to you? Take today and write all the ways you've seen your Father take care of you and your little one.

Thank God for the way you've seen Him work things together for your good (Romans 8:28).

Praise Him for the way you've experienced His presence, especially during this time (Exodus 33:4).

Give Him praise today for His provision (2 Corinthians 9:8).

Thank Him that He knows everything that concerns you (Psalm 138:8).

Momma,

"Love is patient and kind; love does not envy or boast; it is not arrogant or rude. It does not insist on its own way; it is not irritable or resentful; it does not rejoice at wrongdoing, but rejoices with the truth. Love bears all things, believes all things, hopes all things, endures all things" (1 Corinthians 13:4–7). Love keeps no record of wrongs (1 Corinthians 13:5 NIV), so the opposite must be true: love keeps a record of rights. God's perfect definition of love will inspire you to confess that you want to love just like Him. Is your love patient, kind, and longsuffering? He wants to make you just like Jesus, who loved the unlovable, forgave the unforgivable, and gave mercy to the undeserving.

day 273 preference

You may have noticed your baby's preferences in an ultrasound picture, possibly sucking a thumb or waving. God has already designed your little one with a certain tendency toward one hand. That hand will be the dominant one used for writing, catching a ball, and other simple tasks. How neat to discover these sweet little preferences in your child. In the same way, God has uniquely fashioned you and all your ways, righthanded or left, right-brained or left. The way you learn—whether auditorily, visually, or another way—is not an accident or coincidence but rather part of the perfect making of you. Rejoice in who He made you. Rejoice in the way He has made your child.

Thank God for the way He purposes all things in the life of your child (Romans 8:28).

Praise Him for the preferences and tendencies in your little one that make her or him unique. Ask the Father to give your child patience and a submissive heart toward others who may operate differently (Ephesians 5:21).

Pray that your child will love the way God has made them (Psalm 139:14).

Momma,

There's only one you. That's it. God created you with a purpose and destiny unique to you. He is so infinitely creative, and His kingdom requires that you fulfill your special role in advancing it. He didn't make two of you (even if you have an identical twin) because He wants a distinct relationship with you. No copies or imitations. Your life matters, sister. Ask Him today how He wants to bring heaven to earth through you.

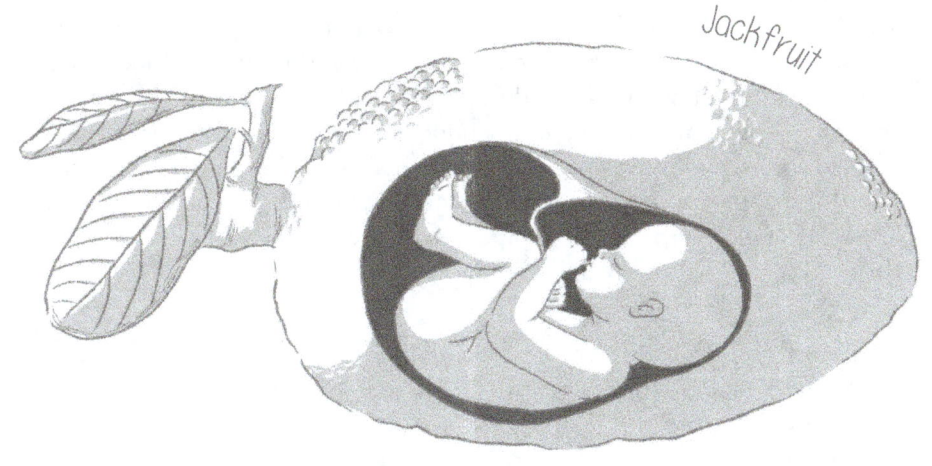

Jackfruit

WEEK

forty

day 274 influence

Did you know your little one's heartrate increases slightly as your heartrate increases? This makes sense because their body is attached by the umbilical cord. You have been your baby's main supply of blood, nutrition, and comfort during these nine months. In the same way you've influenced your little one physically, you are a significant influence spiritually. You've sown hundreds of prayers for your little one so far, and you haven't even met them yet. Keep that prayerful heart as your child grows and matures. The prayers you pray for them are being kept in heavenly bowls (Revelation 5:8).

Ask to be an even greater imitator of God as His beloved child. Pray to walk in love, as Christ loved you and gave Himself up for you (Ephesians 5:1-2).

As your little one grows into a young man or woman, the days can be long. Pray that the Holy Spirit will empower you to not grow weary in discipline and love (Galatians 6:9).

Momma,

Your prayers have great power to produce blessings in the life of your child. No one on earth loves or cherishes them like you. You've been given a unique spiritual authority to pray for them, unlike anyone else in your child's sphere of influence. God has already equipped you with all that is necessary to pray and blanket your little one: His Word and His Spirit. Just imagine your prayers for them echoing throughout all eternity.

day 275   clean

Your natural desire to clean in preparation for the birth, called nesting, has most likely been in full operation for several weeks now. Many mommas experience a feeling that their nests need to be completely ready to bring a baby home. God put the longing for order and cleanliness in you; it speaks of His nature to make all things new. Even nesting is a glory to your Father. Today, as you're steeped in laundry or making freezer meals, praise Him for the perfect way He has made you new.

Welcome the Lord into your baby's room. He said about His temple, "Now my eyes will be open and my ears attentive to the prayer that is made in this place. For now I have chosen and consecrated this house that my name may be there forever. My eyes and my heart will be there for all time" (2 Chronicles 7:15-16).

Thank God that He has built your house and watches over it. "Unless the LORD builds the house, those who build it labor in vain. Unless the LORD watches over the city, the watchman stays awake in vain" (Psalm 127:1).

Momma,

In a few days, your baby will come home. You've dusted and decluttered. You've set up a nursery or other special space with little clothes hanging in the closet. Now you're waiting to see your precious child face-to-face. What a precious foreshadowing of the way Jesus is right now preparing a place for you in heaven (John 14:3). He is making it beautiful just for you. He is longing for the day when He will see you face-to-face.

day 276 perfect

Your little one's exact weight remains a mystery. You may have been told an estimated weight, but for now you can only imagine several pounds of cute baby curled up under your ribs. Spiritually, God has made perfect provisions for your little ones to grow in knowledge of Him. What they will know of Jesus as a toddler will be the foundation for how they will love Him as an adult. Thank God for His wisdom and patience as your child grows.

Pray that your child will grow in grace and knowledge of the Lord (2 Peter 3:18).

Thank God for the way He will feed your child the pure milk of the Word, so that by it, they will grow up in their salvation (1 Peter 2:2-3).

Ask God to fill your child with the knowledge of His will through all wisdom and understanding that the Spirit gives (Colossians 1:9-10).

Momma,

You are well aware that you bear the title "Momma," but you will also take on a new identity very soon: teacher. Your child learns from you daily, watching your responses, listening to your words, and forming ideas that will forever shape their life. Whew! That can seem a little overwhelming unless you rest in this promise: "If any of you lacks wisdom, let him ask God, who gives generously to all without reproach, and it will be given him" (James 1:5). You have everything you need in Him.

day 277 — wait

Any day and hour could signal your baby's birth. You are very close to meeting the little one God has formed for just over thirty-eight weeks. You may be a tad nervous about the unknown. Even if you've had a baby before, you know that each birth is unique. Take some time today to rest in God's perfect love. Just receive. Go ahead and envision your heart opening up to Him like a delicate flower. Picture gentle rain falling from the sky and tapping the petals.

You can be assured that God calls Himself El Roi, "the God Who Sees." He has not taken His adoring eyes off you for a second. You are the apple of His eye (Psalm 17:8).

Ask God to open your spiritual eyes to what He is doing in your heart.

Praise Him that He will empower you to be a vessel of the love He has poured into you (Romans 5:5). You were made to both receive and to give love.

Thank Him that His perfect love casts out fear (1 John 4:18). His love will crush every anxiety and weight about this upcoming birth.

Momma,

The Lord is as excited about this little one as you are. He is such a good Dad, ready to give you this precious gift. Just like the anticipation of children at Christmas, so, too, parents are filled with joy over the presents they've specially picked out. Can you sense His anticipation over your life? He is the best giver, and the gift of parenthood will glorify Him in the way He parents you—full of love, grace, and mercy. "I will be a father to you, and you shall be sons and daughters to me, says the LORD Almighty" (2 Corinthians 6:18).

day 278   bond

You are crossing the pregnancy finish line. Soon your hands will literally hold the goodness of God. Your babies will bond with you like no one else. They will immediately distinguish your voice from all others since it was the very first sound they knew. You, Momma, are that safe place for your child. Your hugs, your kisses, and your snuggles will all be stored up in the heart of your little one. In the same way, God binds His heart to yours at the moment of salvation. He calls you His beloved daughter, forever His. He will be your eternal safe place, and His Spirit will be your comforter. It is His strong arms that wrap around you, embracing you in His love. In Him, you will find all your soul will ever need. He is your heart's perfect provision.

Thank God for His love that binds everything together in perfect harmony (Colossians 3:14).

Praise God for the encouragement, affection, and compassion that are found in Jesus (Philippians 2:1).

God can never forget one of His own, just as you cannot forget your own child (Isaiah 49:15). Rejoice and find security in His love today.

Momma,

Journal the ways He is preparing your heart for the little baby about to come into your life.

day 279 labor

You are anticipating labor any day. You may feel a mix of joyful anticipation and anxiousness about the details of delivery. When will it actually happen? Will you have a smooth labor or complicated one? Most women feel these emotions and have these questions before such a life-altering moment in their lives. Praise God for His peace and grace in the midst of your labor. Spiritually, you often "labor" for growth in the Lord. You may strive in your prayers or even feel frustrated not knowing when God will answer. Take heart, sister. Jesus says to come to Him when you need rest from your labor (Matthew 11:28). Salvation gives you access to His life-giving power in the Spirit.

Praise God for His promise to strengthen you and help you, upholding you with His right hand (Isaiah 41:10).

Jesus acknowledged what you will experience in labor. Thank Him for the joy you are about to experience. John 16:21 says, "When a woman is giving birth, she has sorrow because her hour has come, but when she has delivered the baby, she no longer remembers the anguish, for joy that a human being has been born into the world."

Momma,

Every delivery is different. Some babies are born quickly, while others may take days. You are going to show the amazing way God designed your body! When your cervix dilates to ten centimeters, you're ready for delivery. You've most likely gotten all your details planned, but sometimes your best plans give way to the unanticipated. Trust God for His sufficient grace and He will be glorified through your birth story.

day 280 worship

You're almost there! In anticipation of delivery and labor, you may let your mind slip into questioning the unknown. Your heart may need to refocus on the God who will supply His amazing grace to your calling in motherhood. Worship and praising God will set your mind on things above (Colossians 3:2). You can worship God in many ways by singing, praying, setting aside time to meditate on His love, and being with the body in fellowship. You're not limited to these, but consider how He might call you to worship Him, setting your heart on Him in thankfulness.

"Sing to the LORD, all the earth! Tell of his salvation from day to day. Declare his glory among the nations, his marvelous works among all the peoples!" (1 Chronicles 16:23-24).

"Make a joyful noise to the LORD, all the earth! Serve the LORD with gladness! Come into his presence with singing!" (Psalm 100:1-2).

Offer a sacrifice of praise for this new life inside of you, thanking God for His mighty work in your life (Hebrews 13:15).

Momma,

You will be absolutely smitten with your little one the moment you lay eyes on them. You will be consumed with getting to know this new person and discovering who God created them to be. With so much time spent focused on another, you might be tempted to let the lines blur for true worship. It's possible for you to worship this little one and not realize it. Stay in a place of loving God with a single eye, not letting anything or anyone become the preeminent place of focus in your heart. Your child needs you to love God with all your heart, all your mind, and all your strength (Mark 12:30).

day 281   new

Praise God for His faithfulness. The planet will soon grow by another precious soul. Welcome to the world, little one. May all God's desire come true in your life.

Let Psalm 139 be your prayer over your child:

O Lord, you have searched me and known me!
You know when I sit down and when I rise up;
you discern my thoughts from afar.
You search out my path and my lying down
and are acquainted with all my ways.
Even before a word is on my tongue,
behold, O Lord, you know it altogether.
You hem me in, behind and before,
and lay your hand upon me.
Such knowledge is too wonderful for me;
it is high; I cannot attain it.
Where shall I go from your Spirit?
Or where shall I flee from your presence?
If I ascend to heaven, you are there!
If I make my bed in Sheol, you are there!
If I take the wings of the morning
and dwell in the uttermost parts of the sea,
even there your hand shall lead me,
and your right hand shall hold me.
If I say, "Surely the darkness shall cover me,
and the light about me be night,"
even the darkness is not dark to you;
the night is bright as the day,
for darkness is as light with you.
For you formed my inward parts;
you knitted me together in my mother's womb.
I praise you, for I am fearfully and wonderfully made.
Wonderful are your works;

my soul knows it very well.
My frame was not hidden from you,
when I was being made in secret,
intricately woven in the depths of the earth.
Your eyes saw my unformed substance;
in your book were written, every one of them,
the days that were formed for me,
when as yet there was none of them.
How precious to me are your thoughts, O God!
How vast is the sum of them!
If I would count them, they are more than the sand.
I awake, and I am still with you. ...
Search me, O God, and know my heart!
Try me and know my thoughts!
And see if there be any grievous way in me,
and lead me in the way everlasting!

Momma,

You are officially a mother. You are entering a call from
heaven that will require prayer and dependence on God like
you haven't experienced before. You will also understand His
love for you and see it in ways you may not have before now.
May your heart multiply in grace and joy, from now until you
see Him face-to-face.

About the Author

Marie Lynch is a pastor's wife, homeschooling mom, and wholehearted encourager who loves living as a beloved daughter of God. She wears many hats, but her favorite is a crown. With a background in journalism and professional writing, she has always been passionate about words. Her journey into full-time ministry began in her home, where she embraced the calling of raising and discipling her children.

During her third pregnancy, Marie longed for a resource to help her pray daily over her unborn child. Out of that desire, *Praying in Pregnancy* was born, also fulfilling her dream of writing a book. Over the next decade, between late-night nursing sessions, leading women's ministries, and homeschooling four children, she crafted these daily entries—scribbling prayers and reflections on notebook paper. As the years passed, God expanded her vision for the book: to encourage expectant mothers in any season to see the intentionality of a loving God for every human's life.

When she's not teaching classic literature or hunting for thrifted treasures, Marie finds joy in discipling young women and building up the local church. Through her writing and social media platforms, she serves as a good news anchor, sharing her everyday adventures with the Holy Spirit and inspiring others to find joy in their relationship with God.

Facebook: https://www.facebook.com/marie.lynch.946
Instagram: https://www.instagram.com/marielynch1/

About the Illustrator

Based in Dublin, Ireland, Carole Fannon has worked in the animation industry for quite a few years (enough to stop counting, she says). If her toddler is not pulling the pencil out of her hand, she loves to illustrate, experiment with print, and play around with type. Her other love is that of animals, and these appear quite a lot in her work.

www.ingramcontent.com/pod-product-compliance
Lightning Source LLC
Chambersburg PA
CBHW070547130626
46556CB00001B/48